HOW TO OWN YOUR SH!T

MASTERING SELF-PROJECTION

HOW TO

OWN YOUR

SH!T

MASTERING SELF-PROJECTION

Self-projection is the mask we wear, but self-reflection

is the mirror we need.

Tanya Beauty Coach

DEDICATION

I owe my deepest gratitude to my daughter, as she has
been the foundation of my journey toward self-love.
Additionally, I extend my heartfelt thanks to my mom
for giving me life (twice!) and to my family for their
unwavering support in all my endeavors. I would also
like to give special recognition to my friends Rose K. and
Deepak Chopra for their invaluable guidance on my
path to healing, and last but not least, to my OG's - you
all hold a special place in my heart.
Thank you so much, I love you all xxx.

CONTENTS

INTRO

PERCEPTION OR REALITY

What if I told you that your emotions could be distorting your perception of reality?

In the grand tapestry of existence, where the threads of self-reflection and self-projection intertwine, a remarkable narrative unfolds. Welcome to a world where the depths of our souls are illuminated, and the power to shape our reality resides within. Brace yourself for a captivating journey through the corridors of introspection, where the mirrors of our own perceptions reveal the intricate dance of our true selves. This is not just a book, but an invitation to delve into the depths of your being, to unravel the mysteries that lie beneath the surface. Embark on a transformative odyssey, where self-reflection becomes a portal to profound self-discovery, and self-projection becomes the brush that paints our lives with purpose and authenticity. Prepare to embark on a soul-stirring expedition, where the boundless potential of self-realization awaits at every turn.

I urge you to approach this book not as a passive reader, but as an active participant in your own transformation. Take the ideas and concepts presented here and bring them to life in your own unique way. While my personal anecdotes and experiences may occasionally find their way into the text, they are merely illustrations, signposts pointing the way forward. This book is ultimately about you—the hero of your own story—and the immense potential that awaits when you harness the power within.

Upon my initial exposure to the self-projection theory through the teachings of Carl Jung and Deepak Chopra, I became fixated on the concept as it sparked a strong interest within me. I had so many questions. "Are all my assumptions about others wrong? If what I see in others is a projection of me, where do they come from and why can't I recognize them"? For years, I made it my mission to read, meditate and experience this idea to better understand and apply it. Once I did, it completely changed the way I saw myself and the world. It was emotionally draining at first because it required a lot of self-reflection, redirecting thoughts, and reprogramming my mind but it was all worth it. I was searching for inner peace, and this was the final piece to the puzzle. If I was able to turn my life around emotionally, physically, and spiritually and truly find healing and inner peace, I believe it's a possibility for anyone.

In this book, I will challenge your perceptions, beliefs, and truths. Reading this may stir up uneasy feelings and may disrupt your "comfort zone," however self-awareness and the willingness to get uncomfortable can promote personal growth resulting in a deep sense of inner peace. Get ready to challenge your assumptions and broaden your horizons - "This is owning your sh!t 101."

FROM SURVIVAL TO POTENTIAL

I fully grasped the concept of self-projection in the tranquil embrace of a peaceful morning meditation. With a steaming cup of tea in hand and as the sun's gentle warmth caressed my face, I had a profound revelation—*the key to my lifelong quest for peace lay hidden in the clutches of others' opinions.*

Since childhood, the weight of being labeled as "different" had cast me as an outsider, consumed by the ceaseless worry of how others perceived me. But in that transformative moment, I discovered the truth—how the echoes of their judgments had silently corroded my own happiness. With the first rays of dawn, casting their gentle glow on my face, a resounding whisper echoed within the depths of my consciousness: *"I am infinite potential."* In that precise instant, I transcended the limitations of others' perceptions, realizing that I was not merely defined by their opinions. Moreover, I shed the illusion of my own self-perception, for I was a kaleidoscope of infinite possibilities, constantly evolving and embracing the ever-unfolding tapestry of my being. The truth shimmered before me, radiant and awe-inspiring—I was an extraordinary embodiment of limitless potential, surpassing any preconceived notions or self-imposed constraints. I am infinite! An "ah-ha moment" that I can't fully explain, but so profound that I broke down in tears.

A sense of liberation enveloped me as if a burdensome weight had finally been released. I had been carrying the burden of others' opinions about me for far too long and while I was already acquainted with the concept of projecting one's self-image, it was at that precise moment that I understood its impact. Taking responsibility, in other words, owning your sh!t, involves recognizing how your thoughts and feelings can affect how you view the world. By acknowledging your self-projections and engaging in introspection, you can gain a deeper understanding of yourself. I believe it's never about being perfect, it's just about being aware.

"You are not in the world. The world is in you."
Deepak Chopra

For most of my childhood, I struggled a lot emotionally with depression and anxiety, physically with kidney disease, high blood pressure, migraines, and anemia to name a few. Looking back, my childhood seems like a blur of painful memories mixed with bits and pieces of a few loving ones. I remember feeling tired and sick a lot. I was labeled as a lazy child, unknowing that I had F.S.G.S., a chronic disease that attacks the kidneys. I would take 4-hour naps as a toddler and when most kids grew out of nap time, I would fall asleep everywhere and anywhere any chance I got. Throughout my early years, I experienced a significant amount of emotional, physical, and sexual trauma from various individuals. Although I am not yet prepared to discuss this openly, it is relevant to note that when I reflect on my childhood memories, many of them are associated with pain and suffering. My initial year in high school was no exception. I befriended a girl early in the year who eventually became the leader of a group of about ten bullies. One evening I got a call from this friend who accused me of talking bad about her. I recall feeling stunned as I defended myself by telling her about the lesson my mother had taught me when I was young - to refrain from gossiping and to always speak about others as if they were present in the room. This friend didn't believe me and that's when the bullying started. Throughout the year, this large group of kids would often push me down the hallway stairs, beat me up and verbally abuse me whenever they had the opportunity. I was constantly hiding and frequently sought refuge in the bathroom or library. My grades were declining, and I would cry in class but at the time, teachers did not take much action against bullying and the blame was often placed on the victim, which I still find difficult to comprehend.

There is however a specific memory that stands out to me where the group of kids attempted to burn my hair. After that traumatic incident, I went home in tears and recounted the story to my mom. She was furious and had enough of the bullying. The following day, she met with the principal to discuss the issue, however, his response was dismissive, stating that "kids will be kids" and expressing his satisfaction that he wouldn't have to deal with this anymore since he was retiring that year. The following day his solution was to confiscate the lighter from one of the bullies.

During that time, my parents were separated, and my father had temporarily moved to Jamaica. He returned to visit us about a month after the hair-burning incident and was shocked by the ongoing bullying I had been experiencing throughout the year. He asked me why I didn't stand up for myself, and as someone who was influenced by my Catholic upbringing, I responded that I had to be like Jesus and "turn the other cheek." Whenever I was physically attacked, I would repeat the phrase "Forgive them, Father, for they know not what they do" to myself as a way to cope with the situation. My father shared his exasperation with harmful religious perspectives and emphasized the need for us to take action. He immediately inquired about the identities of the primary bullies and managed to locate them, paying a visit to their parents that same evening. Although he did not disclose the entire encounter, law enforcement officials showed up at our residence that night, and he was required to speak with them privately in the hallway of our apartment building to clarify the matter. Fortunately, they did not arrest him, but the following day at school, I felt as though I had entered a new dimension. Everything was different. For most of the school year I was running from bullies but that day, I was relieved that everyone seemed scared to come close to me, going out of their way to avoid me. One girl even approached me to apologize. Although the situation was eventually resolved, I remained fearful and continued to experience anxiety whenever someone called my name for a few more years. It was not long after that I discovered through blood tests and biopsies that my blood had been slowly poisoning my kidneys since birth. It was then that I fell into a deep depression. Following two suicide attempts in my early teens, my parents and doctors insisted I seek professional help. Although I consulted with various psychiatrists and received numerous medications, I frequently relapsed into a depressive state. Eventually, I got really good at hiding my sad emotions from others, but the pain stayed with me every day.

In 2005, I found out that I was pregnant, but the doctors gave my baby and I very little chance of surviving. Despite their warnings, I decided to go ahead with the pregnancy. Within a month, I was admitted to the hospital for the rest of my pregnancy and could only make occasional visits back home on weekends. I was severely underweight and couldn't hold any food down. Although I was really sick, for the first time in years, I wanted to live. At less than 10% kidney function, I was induced 7 months into the pregnancy, and my daughter came out screaming, which was a good sign! She was only 3 lbs and had to be incubated for a month, but she made it through and has been resilient ever since.

A year after her birth, I was extremely grateful to receive a kidney from my loving mom. However, after the transplant, I went through five more surgeries and had to deal with several health issues that continued to affect my mental health. Nevertheless, at this point in my life, I felt like I finally had a reason to live - my daughter.

"I am not what you think I am.

You are what you think I am."

J. Krishnamurti

In 2007, a glimpse of the beginning of my healing journey started when I embarked on the process of freeing myself from the constraints of my old reality. My emotions prior to that were running the show. I had no control over my thoughts and feelings. What I didn't realize then is I was missing a very big key point: self-awareness.

My encounter with "The Secret," both in book and movie form, authored by Rhonda Byrne, ignited a shift within me. The message that we possess the power to transform our lives through positive thinking and elevating our vibrational energy prompted me to embrace its teachings. For a few years, I tried hard to maintain a cheerful outlook and although I noticed small changes in and around me, I was still struggling on hard days because my health wasn't improving. It was hard to keep smiling while my body was in pain, so I found myself either being very reactive or dismissive to the people I cared most about. Even with the transplant, the blood disease made it extremely hard to do daily tasks. The doctors warned me that this disease could poison the transplanted kidney, so I had fear surrounding my health. Even though I would try to be positive, my body was still sick.

The few books I was reading then said "We create our diseases" so I would start shaming myself when I couldn't heal my body. "Fake it till you make it" didn't work for me and I didn't realize then that not only was I suppressing emotions, but I was also surrounded by people who matched the energy of the hidden self-rejection, inauthenticity, anger, and frustration I had for myself.

In 2009 I was admitted to the hospital for another emergency surgery. The operation went terribly wrong, and I once again fell into a depression. I felt hopeless. No matter what I did to try to be happy, life was kicking my a$$! I was a single mother with PTSD, trauma, and a chronic disease. How could I be positive when my body was in so much pain? How could I not feel guilty when I would have to cancel an outing to the park with my daughter because of how sick I was? I felt like I was missing out on life. I spoke to a neighbor one day about how the positive high-vibration stuff wasn't working for me, and they recommended a new book called: "The Shadow Effect" by Deepak Chopra, Mariam Williamson, and Debbie Ford. A week later, Amazon recommended "The Secret of The Shadow" by Debbie Ford. Well, let me tell you, these books absolutely changed my life! While reading them, I was also given the movie called "What the bleep do we know". When I watched it, I had to pause it multiple times to process all the new complex information. Healing by combining spirituality with science! It wasn't at all about being positive all the time, it was about balance, energy, and awareness.

This was the actual beginning of my healing journey. I started meditating a few times a week, connected with a wonderful and unforgettable holistic psychologist, took reiki and other classes, read many books about energy, attended sound bowl concerts, and started tapping into the artist in me. Best of all, I stopped floating around the surface of my conscious mind and started to dive deep into my subconscious. In other words, I stopped being fake with myself and faced my deepest fears. The journey was long and hard at first, but I made a deal with myself to work on self-care every day. Louise Hay's book & DVD "You can heal your life, was what helped me find balance, gratitude, and self-love.

Growing up, I used to watch television excessively, specifically comedy, to drown my thoughts. I hated commercials because that break would cause me to spiral into a whirlwind of painful feelings. I had no boundaries with people because I believed my feelings didn't matter. I often thought that not only was my existence pointless, but people would be better off without me around. I had a lot of religious people around me growing up that often told me I would go to hell if I didn't make the "right" choices but thankfully my parents would attempt to reassure me with their more open-minded views.

Ever since I can remember, I had so much fear surrounding my existence here on Earth. When my daughter was born, I found a new sense of purpose, but I was concerned about perpetuating the intergenerational trauma patterns that had been passed down. I started the inner journey for her but ended up finding me. Learning to recognize my self-projections helped me find self-compassion, which then led me to heal my physical body. I began incorporating self-nourishing foods into my diet, maintaining a more consistent workout and meditation routine, fostering kind relationships, and treating myself with greater compassion. As a new mother, I knew I couldn't give up and had to do this for myself and my daughter. My main goal for us was to live with love and inner peace, meaning, regardless of what's happening in the outside world, we can accept all emotions as we experience them and live in the present moment. I understood that by embodying this way of life, by learning to love myself unconditionally through life's ups and downs, I could set a powerful example for her to follow.

CHAPTER 1

BECOMING SELF-AWARE

Self-reflection is the process of looking inward and examining our thoughts, feelings, and behaviors. It's an important skill to develop because it can help us gain self-awareness, discover our strengths and weaknesses, and make loving changes in our lives. It gives us the ability to recognize and understand ourselves on a deeper level.

If you are new to self-reflection, you may try this:

Find a calm and comfortable place where you won't be interrupted. Think about a recent situation or event that has been on your mind. It could be something that made you irritated, anxious, hurt, frustrated, or sad. Ask yourself questions about the situation. For example, what happened? How did I feel? What did I do? What could I have done differently?

Be honest with yourself and try to avoid self-criticism. Write down your thoughts and insights on a paper. This can help you organize and track your progress over time. Reflect on your overall patterns and tendencies. Are there any recurring themes in your thoughts or behaviors? Are there areas of your life where you need to make changes or improvements?

Let's say you were really upset about something and started yelling at someone. With self-reflection, you would be able to recognize that you were feeling angry and that your behavior might not be helpful. You could reflect on why you were feeling that way and consider a different way to express your emotions that might not be hurtful towards yourself or the other person.

To grow self-awareness, you must turn your emotions inwards. For example: instead of saying "They are so offensive!" You may say: "I feel offended." The first one is pointing the finger and the other is taking responsibility for your thoughts. Sometimes it's easier to blame others for our own feelings because taking accountability for the judgemental things we feel about others can make us feel like a bad person.

Within the pages of this book, I aim to demonstrate how embracing your self-projections can be an act of self-love. Although it may be tough initially, looking deep into your innermost thoughts and feelings can sometimes stir up strong emotions.

We'll explore your hidden subconscious emotions, and while it might make some of you feel uncomfortable, I've come to realize that being triggered can have a positive impact, depending on your perspective. When we experience a sudden wave of "negative" emotions, instead of feeling powerless, we can reframe the experience and feel excited because we may have uncovered a hidden aspect of ourselves that requires attention. Have you ever offered advice to someone and realized that advice was actually meant for you?

If you have ever felt like you have lost a part of yourself, this can serve as the catalyst for rediscovering your true self. I hope to guide you through your projections with lots of love! I would challenge you to try to get excited when a new uncomfortable feeling surfaces. Think of it as a plot twist in a romantic movie. Right after everything seems to be going wrong, that is often the point where the main character has an epiphany and transforms their life, ultimately finding love, healing, and happiness.
Awareness can be shocking and even a little scary, but it is the first step to healing.

I use a technique for self-awareness with my clients, which I like to call: *3 In, 3 Out, 3 All.* It's a body scan where you become focused and completely aware of what you're feeling physically. You don't try to change what you're feeling, you just "feel" it. Become conscious of your unconscious. The reason for this practice is to just be with yourself. We get so busy from the moment we wake up; we forget to simply listen to our body and validate our emotions. We often get tempted to fix, control and change things that we cannot control. This practice is to reconnect with yourself all while releasing control. Being with you, without judgment. Let's try this together.

For about 3 minutes, sitting or standing, become aware of what you're physically feeling in your body. Don't try to change it, just become aware. Do you feel hot? Cold? Any pressure or pain? Perhaps you feel tingling or vibrations in your hands and feet? Is your stomach growling? Listen to your body and scan it from head to toe. Now for another 3 minutes, become aware of the feelings around your body. Do you feel the clothes on your body? Do you feel the hair on your head? A breeze? Heat? Scan from head to toe. For the last 3 minutes or so, focus your attention both in and all around you. Can you feel the cool air entering your nose as you inhale, and the warm air coming out?

Practice this often and you'll notice a deeper connection with your body. You can also try this when you're in different situations. Stressed, working out, at your job, with children, alone, while eating... You'll start to notice your body is communicating with you, and you will become aware enough to listen.

"Self-awareness is the ability to take an honest look at your life without any attachment to it being right or wrong, good or bad." Debbie Ford

CONSCIOUS WORDS

Before we start, I want to clarify some words I will be using.

The difference between the conscious mind, unconscious mind, the subconscious & consciousness.

Conscious mind: The conscious mind refers to our state of awareness, attention, and focus. It encompasses our capacity for logical and critical thinking. Interestingly, the conscious mind constitutes less than 5 percent of our overall brain function, yet it has the remarkable ability to process approximately 40 to 50 bits of information per second. It is through our conscious mind that we intentionally engage in logical reasoning and analysis.

One notable feature of the conscious mind is its ability to distinguish between the past, present, and future. It enables us to perceive and comprehend the passage of time. As you are presently reading this, it is your conscious mind that is actively involved in the process. The act of reading and comprehending these words is a deliberate choice made by your conscious mind. By emphasizing this mind, we can exercise control over our cognitive processes, directing our attention and focus where we choose. It is through the conscious mind that we engage in intentional thought and decision-making, allowing us to actively shape our experiences and interactions with the world.

Unconscious Mind: Absence of awareness. The unconscious mind refers to the realm of our thoughts, perceptions, and experiences that lie beyond our immediate awareness. It encompasses the aspects of ourselves that we are not consciously aware of, but which can be brought to conscious attention through intentional focus. The unconscious includes various elements such as automatic bodily functions (like breathing), sensory perceptions (such as colors and sounds, stored memories, and even actions like walking.)

Although we may not constantly think about or pay attention to these unconscious processes, when we consciously direct our attention towards them, we can bring them into our conscious awareness. By consciously focusing on something unconscious, like the color of a wall or the sensation of our breathing, we can become more aware of the processing happening within our unconscious mind. Bringing the unconscious into our awareness is a practice that allows us to live more fully in the present moment. By regularly engaging in this process, we can cultivate a greater sense of awareness and mindfulness. Over time, this practice can have positive effects on mental well-being, potentially helping to alleviate symptoms of depression and anxiety.

Subconscious Mind: Absence of awareness. The subconscious mind refers to the vast realm of our mental processes that operate below our conscious awareness. It is constantly active even when we are asleep. Remarkably, the subconscious mind accounts for over 95 percent of our brain function and processes a staggering 11 million bits of information per second.

One crucial aspect of the subconscious mind is its role in housing our hidden emotions. It serves as a sort of "storage facility" or "database" for the emotions associated with our current and past experiences, as well as our memories. Operating in a present-based manner, the subconscious does not differentiate between the past, present, or future; it simply stores and processes emotions without intention or conscious control. Moreover, the subconscious mind is responsible for generating unintentional feelings, behaviors, habits, dreams, thoughts, and actions. As you are reading this, your brain is actively processing every scent, color, and texture of the environment around you, even if your conscious mind remains unaware of it. Reflecting on this phenomenon can indeed be quite overwhelming.

To move from the subconscious to the conscious, information must traverse the realm of the unconscious mind. The unconscious mind acts as a bridge, allowing the subconscious to surface into conscious awareness. It's important to note that the subconscious mind plays a significant role in processing and storing the emotions associated with our experiences. This process contributes to our Emotional self-projections. Unlike the conscious mind, the subconscious operates beyond our control, without the ability to choose.

Consciousness: The term "consciousness" can be used in different contexts, leading to varying interpretations. In the context of subjective experience and awareness, consciousness refers to our cognitive and perceptual faculties.

On the other hand, when consciousness is referred to as the soul or spirit, it takes on a more spiritual connotation. In this sense, consciousness represents the deeper essence of our being, the core aspect that transcends physical existence. It is associated with the idea of an eternal, immaterial aspect of ourselves that persists beyond the limitations of the physical body. In this book I will be using the concept of **consciousness as the soul or spirit**. Basically, the energy within you that makes your body "alive."

"We don't see things as they are, we see them as we are." Anais Nin

CHAPTER 2

WHAT IS SELF-PROJECTION

Self-projections are both positive and negative emotions, beliefs, qualities, faults, opinions, judgments, and even sometimes behaviors that we see in another that we possess.

The concept of "projection" in psychology has been discussed by several prominent psychologists, including Sigmund Freud and Carl Jung.

Freud, the founder of psychoanalysis, proposed the idea of projection in his work on defense mechanisms. According to Freud, projection involves attributing one's own unacceptable or unwanted thoughts, feelings, or impulses to another person. This defense mechanism allows individuals to distance themselves from their own undesirable traits and project them onto others. Jung, a Swiss psychiatrist, and psychoanalyst wrote extensively about projection throughout his career, beginning in the early 1900s and continuing until his death in 1961. His ideas on projection are included in several of his major works, including "Psychological Types" (1921), "The Archetypes and the Collective Unconscious" (1959), and "Two Essays on Analytical Psychology" (1953).

He suggested that projection involves attributing one's own desires or motivations onto others and that it can be a way of confronting and integrating aspects of the self that have been repressed. So, while neither Freud nor Jung can be credited with "inventing" the concept of projection, they both made significant contributions to our understanding of this psychological phenomenon.

"Everything that irritates us about others can lead us to an understanding of ourselves. Everyone is our mirror. Our reflections in others show us not only who we are, but also how to be better." Carl Jung

When we project onto others our feelings, opinions, and assumptions about them without self-reflection, without realizing it is coming from our mind and emotions, not recognizing it in ourselves may be a protection mechanism, protecting ourselves from uncomfortable feelings. It can be too hard to face those aspects within us, so instead, we project them onto others. In many cases a sort of denial of the self. Here are some examples of negative projections:

-A dishonest person may frequently accuse others of being deceitful, even when there is no evidence to support this claim. This could be a way for the person to distance themselves from their own dishonesty by projecting it onto others.

-Someone who is struggling with feelings of anger may project these emotions onto others by assuming that people around them seem often angry, even if there is no objective evidence to support this belief.

-A person who is insecure about their attractiveness may project their insecurities onto others by assuming that people are judging them negatively based on their appearance, even if there is no evidence to support this.

In each of these examples, the person is projecting their own thoughts, feelings, or motivations onto others, which can create misunderstandings or conflict in their relationships with others.

Examples of positive projections:

A person who has a positive self-concept may project their own positive qualities onto others, assuming that others are kind, trustworthy, and honest, which can lead to either positive interactions and relationships with others or feeling deceived when the other person is not what they assumed them to be.

Someone who has a growth mindset and believes that they can improve their skills and abilities may project this belief onto others, assuming that others are also capable of learning and growth.

TYPES OF SELF-PROJECTIONS

I've named and placed them in 4 categories:

- **Emotional Self-Projections:** Refers to the process by which we subconsciously attribute positive and negative emotions and assumptions towards others that actually reflect our own feelings towards ourselves. To describe this type, people often use adjectives. Throughout our lives, Emotional self-projections persist. While they can change and transform as we develop self-awareness and experience personal growth, the underlying tendency to externalize our internal emotions remains consistent. In practical terms, Emotional self-projections manifests as assumptions that are not necessarily based on factual information. It can also be seen through criticisms or compliments that we direct towards others, which ultimately reveal our own inner judgments or affirmations about ourselves. *How I feel about you is actually how I feel about me.*

- **Presumption Self-Projection:** This type occurs when we mistakenly presume that others possess the same feelings, outlooks, and perspectives as we do, leading to a false sense of awareness. It becomes evident when we experience a triggered response when someone disagrees with our beliefs or values, as we expect them to share our emotional state. Presuming others have the same preferences for tastes and hobbies, or share the same opinions, such as sports teams, religious or political views, are examples of Presumption self-projection. It's important to note that since this type resides in the unconscious, once we become aware of this tendency, we gain the ability to stop it. *I assume you are feeling what I am feeling*.

- **Knowledge Self-Projections**: This type arises from the unconscious assumption that others possess the same abilities and/or knowledge as ourselves, leading to a false sense of awareness. Knowledge self-projections appear when we get triggered if someone fails to excel at the same abilities or share the knowledge that we possess. It is important to note that this type of self-projection is not constant , and once we become aware of it, we have the capacity to stop it. Examples of knowledge self-projections include instances where a plumber assumes that everyone should know how to repair pipes, a basketball player assumes that everyone can dribble a ball, or a highly intellectual person assumes that everyone shares their level of knowledge. *I assume you know what I know.*

- **Absolved Self-Projection**: This type is characterized by the denial of one's own behaviors, attitudes, and actions, which are instead projected onto others in a reversed manner. Unlike other types of projections that stem from our emotions, this type revolves around our own actions and conduct. It involves absolving ourselves of responsibility. This type of self-projection can occur both consistently and intermittently so when we become aware that our own actions are being projected, we have the ability to cease them. However, in cases where denial is deeply ingrained in our subconscious, we may be unable to recognize the projection. It is important to note that Absolved self-projection does not apply when factual evidence proves otherwise. Examples include instances where a person who lies or cheats assumes others are lying or cheating on them or others, or when someone hides or denies their own attraction towards someone and assumes that the other person is attracted to them. Additionally, abusers who accuse others of being abusive exhibit this type of projection. *I deny my actions and behaviors and assume you act and behave that way.*

WE ARE THE PROJECTOR

Perceptions play a big part in owning our sh!t. Understanding how we perceive the world and others is the first step to finding out where self-projections come from. What I feel about you is actually what I feel about myself. How is this true? Well, we must first acknowledge that our mind is creating this perception about someone else. If it comes from our minds, why does it have to be true for them? Our reality is based on our perceptions. Our mind creates perceptions about ourselves, others, and the world, therefore the perception belongs to us because again, it came from our mind. We are experiencing life as we are. Some perceptions may have originated from our parents or societal standards, but we have internalized them and now view the world through that lens.

Picture a projector in a movie theater. The projector in the back of the theater is projecting an image onto a screen facing it. The image on the screen is what we see, but the information from that image comes from the actual projector. Your external reality is being processed by your internal reality.

"The whole world is simply my story, projected back to me on the screen of my own perception. All of it."
Byron Katie

Our senses are the gateway to our perceptions, and they allow us to experience life in its entirety. Whether it's tasting food, listening to music, touching objects, smelling fragrances, or seeing the colors of the world, our senses are what enable us to fully engage with the reality around us. Each of us experiences life uniquely through our senses. For instance, what tastes delicious to one person may be repulsive to another, and what one hears may sound slightly different to another. Thus, we are all perceiving reality differently based on our individual experiences, and this shapes our unique "perception of reality."

Suppose you and I are standing near a car, and the car alarm goes off. We will perceive the sound differently depending on our respective positions, attention, and hearing ability. This example highlights that our perception is influenced by various factors. Similarly, when we meet someone, the way we experience them is influenced by our position, attention, and hearing. Regardless of where we stand, we are missing out on certain perspectives and information. The true reality can't be gathered by our one perspective.

We also perceive reality from our emotions. For example, my experiences with my aunt may be quite different from the experiences my cousins had with their mother. My perceptions may cause me to have a different opinion of her compared to others. My emotions towards my aunt and their emotions toward their mother (the same person) will be vastly different.

I had a very loving, fun relationship with my aunt Gaby. She passed away in 2022 and at her funeral, I was asked to speak. I told everyone how authentic she was and how she always made me feel like I didn't have to change who I was to be loved and accepted. That was my perception of her. When my cousins and other people spoke about her, they had many different stories and opinions of her that were interesting to hear, some wild and some more serious. I knew that we all had our experiences with her and that's what created our perceptions. We all had different opinions about the same person. Were they factual? Perhaps! But I'm sure she was much more than what any of us perceived her to be.

Our thoughts continuously create emotions. For example, if you think of a person in your life, the thought of that person will create a feeling inside of you. YOU are the one experiencing that emotion. Try this: think of a person in your life who gets on your nerves. Oh yeah, THAT person! Got them in mind? The thought of that person probably comes with a few choice feelings—annoyance? Frustration? Resentment? Straight-up anger? If I were to ask someone else to think about that same person, they may have a different emotion about them. If I were to ask you: how do you feel about that person? You are experiencing them based on your perceptions. You may create an opinion from your perception. Ask yourself. Have I ever felt that way about myself? When you sit with that uncomfortable feeling, you may discover that it isn't about them. It never is about other people. We experience our emotions, and nobody knows how we feel but ourselves. This is the beginning of owning your sh!t.

Let's expand our perceptions together:

The way to start healing is to become aware of our perceptions and we do this by using our senses to their full potential! Try doing this often throughout your day.

Hyperfocus on a specific sense. Sound for example: Stop reading for a minute and listen to a subtle sound around you. What do you hear? Now hyperfocus and listen to the sounds further away. What do you hear now?

Do you know what just happened? Your brain just stopped thinking of yesterday and tomorrow! You probably even for a second forgot you were reading this book! You became extremely present in this moment.

Let's do some more. Try becoming aware of the objects around you. Describe out loud or in your mind, the colors, and textures.

You may even try this when you are eating, become aware of the smells and tastes. Describe what you're experiencing. What do the textures feel like on your tongue? Is it sweet, sour, or bitter?

I would suggest trying this multiple times a day. The more you program your brain to use your senses to their full potential you are reprogramming your mind to live in the present moment.

Your brain is processing everything that surrounds you and what's within you, unconsciously and subconsciously. When you start using your senses you're not thinking about yesterday or what may happen tomorrow. You're fully living in the now. If you have feelings of stress, anxiety, depression, or hopelessness, you'll notice a shift within you, a trust in the process of life will develop. You will understand that the purpose of life is to simply experience.

WHEN DO SELF-PROJECTIONS START

From birth to about seven years old, we absorb our surroundings like sponges, taking in everything around us and recording it. During this period, we are highly impressionable, and our emotions can change quickly. We are not yet capable of projecting our thoughts and beliefs onto others. Our brain waves during this time are in theta, which is a lower vibrational frequency. When we imagine, meditate, or undergo hypnosis, we also enter a theta state, which is between wakefulness and sleep. In this state, we are fully present in the moment and not yet able to project our thoughts and beliefs onto others. Children are not the projector; they are the experience.

As we get older, we become more aware and function regularly on beta brain waves. Beta is alertness, thinking, processing, and analyzing information. We start creating opinions, judgments, and beliefs after 7. This is the time when we start self-projecting. When we hear something, we tend to internalize it and create beliefs based on the information we've received. Some of these beliefs come from our own experiences, while others come from the perspectives of others. As we continue to absorb information even after childhood, our beliefs are reinforced and start to shape our reality. In a sense, we are both recording and playing back the images from our experiences and perceptions in our visible reality. We become the projector.

Notice a child's simplistic emotions. If they are sad, they cry, if angry they yell, happy they smile, excited they laugh. Their perceptions can change from moment to moment because they're simply experiencing life as it is happening to them. They are using their senses and intuition to guide them through life. But here is the caveat, they are also using other people's feelings, their suggestions, their teachings, and even facial expressions to guide them.

My mother used to talk to me about her interest in the simplicity of young children's emotions when she began studying early childhood development. When my daughter was little, I remember my mother recounting interesting facts she learned from school, and she would share them with me. One day, as my toddler gazed up at me after dropping food on the floor, my mother pointed out that my daughter might be looking for validation or seeking my response on how to react to this event. It made me realize how children often seek our approval and reassurance, wanting to feel secure and validated in their actions and experiences. As my daughter got older and started testing my boundaries, my mom mentioned that this is a great sign of healthy human behavior because young children are realizing slowly that they are separate from their parents. After 18 months old they start having a sense of self, so they will start to say no and act what some people call as defiant, when in fact they are simply starting to follow their own intuition and inner guidance.

It can be easy to live consciously (holding back words and reactions) amongst adults, in the workplace and even amongst friends for a limited amount of time. But because children are naturally vulnerable, we can become vulnerable with them. We may be more comfortable with our emotions around our children. If we meet them with the unaware unhealed vulnerable parts, oftentimes we may find ourselves projecting our sh!t onto them. Our filters aren't on around our kids, so we won't pretend to "feel good" around them like we do around others. When we are tired, upset, or sick feeling our self-projections are in full force, and we unfortunately can end up self-projecting all 4 categories onto them.

Here are some examples of what that may sound like:
Emotional Self-Projection: You are so sensitive! (I may feel like I'm too sensitive and dislike that part of myself.)

Presumption Self-Projection: You should like spaghetti, it's delicious! (I'm assuming they like what I like.)

Knowledge Self-Projection: You should know how to tie your shoes! (I'm assuming they know something I know.)

Absolved self-projection: You are so violent! (Reversing actions, I'm actually violent toward them or others.)

"The particular egoic patterns that you react to most strongly in others and misperceive as their identity tend to be the same patterns that are also in you, but that you are unable or unwilling to detect within yourself."

Eckhart Tolle

CHAPTER 3

FACTS AND SELF-PROJECTIONS

A fact is a statement that can be proven or verified to be true, based on objective evidence, research, observations, or measurements. Facts are not influenced by personal beliefs, opinions, or biases, but are instead grounded in objective reality.

Examples of facts include: Water freezes at 0 degrees Celsius (32 degrees Fahrenheit). The capital of France is Paris. The human body is made up of cells. These are all statements that can be verified through scientific inquiry or other forms of objective evidence.

Emotions are not present when stating facts. Opinions and judgments, on the other hand, are subjective expressions of belief, preference, or evaluation that may or may not be supported by facts. For example, the fact that "Mount Everest is the tallest mountain in the world" is an objective truth that can be verified through scientific observation and measurement. However, whether someone likes me or not is a matter of personal opinion that cannot be proven true or false. Similarly, a judgment about someone's character or behavior is subjective and based on personal values and beliefs, whereas a factual statement about that person's actions or achievements can be verified through evidence. While opinions and judgments can be valuable and informative, it is important to distinguish them from facts in order to make informed decisions and arguments based on evidence and reason. How can we determine the difference? Well, I believe it's by owning what we project.

Self-Projections have to do with the feelings behind what we're saying. More often than not we express emotion when judging or forming an opinion. Sometimes when I form an opinion about someone it may seem that I am right! For example, if I think a person is annoying and many people have the same opinion as me, just because others agree, it still does not make it a fact. Popularity and emotions don't mean factual.

The feeling is still coming from my mind. Emotional self-projections are constant whether we feel we are "right" about them or not.

Interpretation of fact is also not fact. An interpretation of fact is a subjective understanding or explanation of a particular set of factual information. It is different from the factual information itself, but rather, a person's understanding or perspective on that information. Here is an example of an interpretation of fact:

Fact: A man was seen walking out of a store with a television. Interpretation: The man was stealing the television. While the fact in this example is that a man was seen walking out of a store with a television, the interpretation of that fact is that the man was stealing it. However, it is possible that the man had purchased it legally and was simply carrying it out of the store. Therefore, the interpretation is not necessarily a fact, but rather a subjective understanding of the situation based on the available information.

Yes, facts can change. For example, the idea that atoms were dense was a widely held belief in the early 20th century. However, in 1911, Ernest Rutherford and his colleagues conducted the gold foil experiment, which demonstrated that atoms were mostly empty space with a very small and dense nucleus at their center. The facts about an Atom changed without emotion and with new verified information.

If you're wondering if you are self-projecting, make sure you have the facts. I will give examples of fact versus projection using the 4 types:

Fact: My neighbor lost his job last year and hasn't been working.
Emotional Self-Projection: My neighbor is a loser because he doesn't have a job.

Fact: My neighbor's child plays soccer with my child.
Presumption Self-Projection: My neighbor probably likes sports because he put his kid in sport like I did, and I like sports.

Fact: My neighbor doesn't have his driver's license.
Knowledge Self-Projection: My neighbor should know how to drive, it's so easy.

Fact: My neighbor raised his voice at his wife.
Absolved Self-Projection: My neighbor is an abuser. Verifying facts is important, especially for the Absolved self-projection type because strong accusations without facts can be damaging to people. If a person has hurt you or someone verbally, emotionally, or physically you are stating that fact. In that case, it is not an absolved self-projection. If you make assumptions about many people without facts, you may be abusive and cannot recognize it.

CAN WE STOP PROJECTING

Many people have asked me how to stop self-projecting and I personally believe we can't stop the Emotional Projections. These are constant because they come from our subconscious.

Emotions are complex psychological and physiological responses to different stimuli and experiences, such as joy, sadness, anger, fear, and love. They serve as important signals that provide us with information about our environment and help us make decisions. While some people may wish to suppress or avoid certain emotions, it is not possible to completely stop feeling them so evidently, we cannot stop self-projecting them. Attempting to suppress our feelings can be detrimental to our mental and physical health, as emotions play a significant role in our overall well-being and can provide valuable information about ourselves and our environment. When we learn healthy ways of processing and expressing our feelings, our Emotional projections can subconsciously change to become kinder and more loving. As we heal ourselves, we develop a greater sense of self-care and self-love. When we prioritize our own well-being and value ourselves, we tend to become less judgmental of others, consequently, our assumptions and opinions towards others may change, therefore changing what we are projecting.

The quote I always say is "as within so without", which means, whatever you feel on the inside about yourself will radiate onto your outside world. An Emotional Self-Projection is simply you assuming things about others that you actually feel about yourself.

Here's the good news! We can stop the other 3 types: Presumption, Knowledge, and Absolved projections. They reside in the unconscious mind. Referring back to the definition I gave you at the beginning when we become aware of unconscious feelings and actions, we bring them to our conscious mind. When we think logically, we can make changes, which means, if we bring those projections to our awareness and take accountability, we can stop assuming that others are acting or feeling how we are in fact acting or feeling!

Here's an example of how we can become aware:

Let's say your pet peeve is "interrupters." Those people who won't let you get a word in! What if I told you that interrupting may be an Absolved self-projection? Yes, you may be right, and some people do interrupt but if this irritates you, that means it holds a "negative" space within you. The question would then be: have you ever interrupted? That specific projection can stop when you notice you may also be doing it! Perhaps you only interrupt when a subject inspires you. It may not be often, but you can sometimes interrupt, just like the person that irritated you. Now, this is the "cool" part! When you catch that projection and become aware, you will notice a shift in your thoughts, feelings, and actions. When you notice yourself interrupting you may pause and realize that listening may be important now. Additionally, because you are aware that you can sometimes also interrupt, when you hear someone interrupting you, instead of feeling irritated you may change your thought from "That's annoying!" To: "He seems passionate about this subject!"

Question from social media:

Momsflannel: *When your self-projection changes to a positive space, does it affect your circle of people?*

Answer: *The awareness of your self-projection can help reduce the intensity of the emotion behind them. Awareness of them raises our level of consciousness and by owning our projections we gain a deeper understanding and compassion for ourselves and others. We value ourselves and may not feel comfortable with people who are constantly projecting their emotions onto us, so we start setting healthy boundaries. Those who don't respect our boundaries will be filtered out, so yes, I believe this does affect our circle of people.*

PROJECTING BEAUTY

I often have people asking me why they see the beauty and good in others but can't see the good in themselves.

When we recognize someone's beauty or charming and confident demeanor, it may reflect something dormant within us that we are seeking or recognizing in the other person. Sometimes we unconsciously seek qualities in others that we believe we lack. While one person may see someone's charm and confidence as attractive, another may find those same qualities annoying or jealousy-inducing. However, in both cases, the subconscious feeling is the same: a dormant feeling of charm and confidence within ourselves. Therefore, whether we find someone's confidence appealing or irritating, it is ultimately a reflection of our own thoughts and feelings about ourselves.

Self-projection isn't just the "uncomfortable" feelings." It's ALL feelings. This principle also applies to projections such as beauty, kindness, and love. Similar to how some individuals struggle to acknowledge their own "negative" judgments and opinions, others may be unaware of their own "positive" qualities. However, if you are able to recognize these qualities in others, it is likely that you possess them within yourself as well, but they are buried in your subconscious. As I've mentioned before, we are only able to perceive in others what we already possess within ourselves. When you project the beauty in others, ask yourself, what do I feel is beautiful about me, and what in me may be stopping me from recognizing it in myself?

Exercise:

Positive Projections.

Think about someone you like. On a piece of paper, write a few qualities you see in them (adjectives).

This is subconsciously something you feel about yourself! Do you remember a time when you felt that about you?

If you struggle to recognize the beauty in yourself, here are some tips to help you get started:

Practice self-care: Taking care of yourself physically, mentally, and emotionally can help you feel better about yourself. This can include things like eating well, getting enough sleep, exercising regularly, and doing activities that bring you joy.

Challenge your critical self-talk. We all have disapproving thoughts about ourselves from time to time, but it's important to challenge them and reframe them in a more positive light. Whenever you catch yourself thinking negatively about yourself, try to reframe the thought into something loving.

Focus on your strengths. Everyone has strengths and talents, so try to focus on what you're good at and what makes you unique. Write them down and remind yourself of them regularly.

Surround yourself with love. Surround yourself with people who lift you up and make you feel good about yourself. This can include friends, family, pets, or even online communities.

Practice gratitude. Take time each day to think about the things you're grateful for, including the good things about yourself. This can help shift your focus to the loving aspects of your life and yourself. Remember, seeing the beauty in yourself is a journey, and it's okay if it takes some time to get there. Be patient with yourself and keep working on it, and you'll start to see the results.

Sometimes we have a tough time feeling positive about ourselves. Our conscious mind can be programmed from our past to reject kind, loving words because of previous experiences that have shaped our beliefs and thought patterns. For example, if someone grew up in an environment where they were constantly criticized or received negative feedback, they may have developed a belief that they are not worthy of love or kindness. In this case, when someone offers them kind and loving words, their conscious mind may reject it because it conflicts with their deeply ingrained belief system. Additionally, the human brain can have a negativity bias, which means that it may tend to give more weight to negative experiences than positive ones. This bias can cause us to overlook or discount positive feedback, even if it is genuinely offered with kindness and love. Ultimately, our past experiences, beliefs, and biases can all contribute to how we receive and respond to kind and loving words in the present. Our conscious mind can deny our true feelings, but our subconscious will always tell the truth through our self-projections.

"Is there a difference between happiness and inner peace? Yes. Happiness depends on conditions being perceived as positive; inner peace does not."
Eckhart Tolle

CHAPTER 4

THE SUBCONSCIOUS

Imagine yourself holding a large bag filled with items. You carry around this bag everywhere you go. The opening to the bag is very narrow so you can't see inside it.

The only way to find out what's in that bag is to put your hand in it and trust that what's in it won't hurt you. Once you pull out what's in the bag and become aware, you now have two choices: #1 Put it back in the bag. #2 Acknowledge it. You can live without knowing what's in there but the longer you hold that full bag, the heavier it will get.

I want you to picture that bag like your subconscious, the part that makes up over 95% of your brain function. Picture that stuff inside the bag as your hidden emotions. Many people are too scared to dig their hands in that bag "the subconscious" fearing what they will find. If you choose to not become aware of your feelings over time you will feel the weight of them. When we ignore our hidden emotions, we teach our minds to suppress what makes us uncomfortable.

When a positive projection comes out, I become aware that I'm feeling confident or self-loving. When a negative one comes out, I realize I have some healing work to do. I don't criticize myself when my projections are "negative", I get excited that my subconscious wants to tell me something.

Self-projecting isn't a "bad" thing. It is a way to discover how we truly feel about ourselves. When you become aware of them you can react with: "Oh no that's terrible!" or get excited that you've just uncovered something hidden. And now that you're aware of it you can find tools to either learn to love those things about yourself or release them because they no longer serve you. **So, inner peace is never about being perfect, it's about being aware.**

SHADOW SELF

The concept of the shadow-self originated with psychologist Carl Jung. The shadow is a term used to describe the hidden aspects of the personality that the conscious mind has repressed or rejected, often due to social conditioning, trauma, or other factors. These repressed aspects of the self can include qualities, desires, and impulses that are considered socially unacceptable, shameful, or negative. According to Jung, it is crucial to recognize and integrate our shadow selves in order to achieve psychological completeness and individualization. He maintained that by making the unconscious aspects of ourselves conscious, we can confront and resolve inner conflicts, increase self-awareness, and ultimately lead more satisfying lives. Since Jung's time, the concept of the shadow self has been widely accepted and developed by other psychologists, therapists, coaches, and spiritual leaders. Today, it is a commonly used idea in the fields of self-improvement and personal development.

It's important to understand that making mistakes or exhibiting certain negative behaviors does not define one's entire identity. For example, telling a lie does not make someone a liar, and acting controlling in a certain situation does not make someone a controller. Similarly, lacking compassion in a particular moment does not necessarily make someone   toxic. We all have different shades of personality that can be positive or negative at various times in our lives. It's unrealistic to expect anyone to be perfect, constantly exuding happiness, despite what social media may convey. While positive emotions are desirable, it's important to acknowledge that we all experience a range of emotions in our physical and emotional existence. The reality is, we have to make peace with duality.

Duality refers to the concept that there are two contrasting, complementary, or interconnected aspects or elements that make up a whole. It is often used in philosophy and spirituality to describe the nature of reality, consciousness, and existence. In the context of duality, these two aspects are often seen as opposing or contradictory, such as light and dark, good, and evil, yin and yang, or masculine and feminine. However, they are also seen as complementary and interdependent, with one aspect needing the other to exist and balance the whole. We have to make peace with the contrast of night and day, darkness, and light, and all the pleasant feelings and all the unpleasant feelings within us.

Picture yourself standing in a dimly lit large room with a lamp located in a corner. As you approach closer to the light, the intensity of your shadow deepens. You can see everything in the room, including your shadow. However, if you walk too far away from the light into the darker part of the room you may become disoriented in the darkness and lose sight of what's in the room. Similarly, if you approach the light and cling to it, the surrounding area becomes obscure, and you will lose sight of things, grasping the light will make the room become dark. So, whether you are too close to the light or too far from it, it can hinder your judgment and situational awareness.

Overall, this metaphor is highlighting the importance of balance and perspective. It suggests that too much or too little of anything can be detrimental, and that we should strive to find a balance that allows us to see things clearly and navigate our environment effectively.

We can compare this analogy to suppressing the subconscious mind. The closer we get to the light the bigger the shadow. The more positive we try to become; the more darkness will surround us. The more negative we become the more darkness will surround us. So, although our awareness (conscious mind) is looking at this beautiful bright light, the fact is, behind us is a huge shadow (subconscious). Too positive or too negative can make us lose awareness.

I'm not crazy about how society uses the words positive and negative when it comes to emotions. In society, positive means good, and negative means bad. For energy to circulate inside a battery, we need both positive and negative energy. We do not think one side of the battery is good and one is bad. We know that both are needed for energy to flow. The same applies to our emotions. Positive (sun, light) gives us energy, vitamins, and healing. Negative (moon, dark) gives us rest, repair, and healing. I've worked with countless amounts of people that tried so hard to be positive and suppress the negative, therefore not owning their self-projections and they all found themselves losing important relationships or things that they valued in their lives. Unawareness can cause a disconnect between ourselves and others. I believe humans above all thrive in vulnerability and authenticity. To create true connections with others, vulnerability is essential. I understand authenticity is one of the hardest things to live by because it means being okay with being flawed.

Spending prolonged periods under the sun can cause various adverse effects such as dehydration, sunburn, headaches, and loss of energy. On the other hand, remaining isolated in darkness can lead to a deficiency of vital vitamins, resulting in low energy and depression. However, maintaining a balance of both the energizing warmth of the sun and taking breaks in the shade to rest, heal, and sleep can create a harmonious equilibrium in our body, mind, and soul. Similarly, constantly maintaining a positive attitude can make it challenging to empathize with others and ourselves when experiencing intense or contrasting emotions. This can turn into "toxic positivity." This term is characterized by an excessive focus on positive thinking and avoiding any acknowledgment of negative feelings or experiences. Toxic positivity can be harmful because it can invalidate or dismiss the genuine experiences and emotions of others, making them feel as if their feelings or experiences are not valid or important. It can also create pressure to always maintain a positive facade, which can be exhausting and unrealistic. For instance, in the event of a loss of a loved one, it is natural to feel sad or grieve, and suppressing those feelings would deny a fundamental aspect of human nature. Have you ever seen a baby without tears? We would never tell a baby to be positive when they cry, so why do we think it's ok to tell adults to not be negative? There are no such thing as negative babies, just babies with emotions.

If you don't like negative emotions, I would ask you "At what age did you start judging your negative feelings?" We cannot fully experience the gratitude of the good times without contrasting feelings to remind us of what the opposite feels like. The same goes for being stuck in uncomfortable emotions. Balance is key.

To overcome toxic positivity, it is important to recognize that it is healthy and normal to experience a range of emotions, including negative ones, and that it is okay to acknowledge and express these feelings. It is crucial to practice self-compassion and empathy towards oneself and others and to create space for authentic emotions and experiences without judgment.

When I do shadow work with my clients one of the number one most important aspect of uncovering your shadow self is owning your self-projections. Shadow work involves bringing these unconscious aspects of ourselves into conscious awareness, acknowledging and accepting them, and incorporating them into our personality. This process can involve various techniques such as self-reflection, journaling, meditation, coaching, therapy, and other forms of inner work.

A lot of people believe that we have to heal the shadow when in fact we simply must integrate it. But because of society, our parents, and our friend's standards, over time, we do end up pushing away all the things that we don't like about ourselves. We push them down to our subconscious and create dark shadows that come out sometimes as self-projections. What I see in you is a reflection of me.

Finding our shadow through our projections exercise:

Think back to the last time that someone got on your nerves or offended you.

- What happened? Jot down the event in one or two sentences.
- Describe the other person's behavior using 1-3 adjectives. Examples: inconsiderate, selfish, childish...

- Can you think of an occasion where you behaved that way yourself? Note it down in 1-2 sentences.

One way to identify the parts of your shadow self that you dislike is to pay attention to what you dislike in others. By recognizing similar feelings or traits in other people that you find unappealing, you can begin to uncover the aspects of yourself that you may be trying to repress or deny. What are some of the shadow qualities or traits that you dislike or struggle with?

Emotional Self-Projections: (things I disapprove of) What did I feel about another that I actually felt about myself?

Presumption Self-Projections: What did I assume others liked or disliked that I myself liked or disliked?

Knowledge Self-Projections: What ability did I expect others to excel or be good or bad at that I myself am good or bad at?

Absolved Self-Projections: What action or behaviors did I assume others where doing, that in actuality I was doing?

Remember this exercise isn't about fixing anything it's just about self-reflection. Being self-aware is crucial for several reasons. Firstly, it helps us to identify our strengths and weaknesses, understand our values, beliefs, and motivations, and recognize areas where we may need to improve. This knowledge is essential for personal growth and integrating our shadow selves. Secondly, self-awareness helps us to make better decisions. By understanding our values and motivations, we can make decisions that align with our goals and avoid making decisions based on emotions or biases. Thirdly, self-awareness improves our relationships with others. By recognizing our own emotions and behaviors, we can communicate more effectively, resolve conflicts more successfully, and form stronger, more meaningful relationships.

Try to embrace and integrate your shadow self into your personality. Recognize that these parts of yourself are a natural and normal part of being human.

"Everyone sees other people differently because everyone is projecting aspects of him or herself."
Debbie Ford

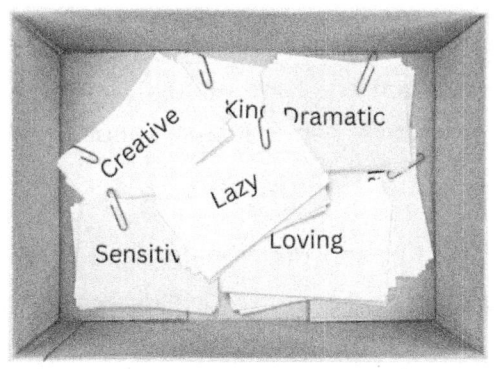

WHAT'S IN MY BOX?

We all hold a metaphorical box filled with labels of who we think we are. We aren't even what is in that box, these are just things we picked up along the way of our life journey. As we grow up, we learn about what's valued as "good" and what's not, we pick up information from our family, friends, movies, television, and social media. Over time our box slowly starts to fill up with our own feelings, expectations, opinions, and emotions about ourselves. Here are some examples of self-loving traits that may be in someone's box: I am a hard worker, I am capable of achieving my goals, I am a good listener, I am intelligent and capable of learning new things, I am a caring and empathetic person.

Here are some examples of self-critical traits that may be in someone's box: I am not good enough, I always mess things up, I am not attractive, I am not smart enough, It's always my fault.

If while growing up and developing your sense of self, you were surrounded by people who had loving, kind things to say, chances are your box is filled with loving emotions, thoughts, and opinions, and the opposite happens if you have people criticize and judge you. Unfortunately, when we are the recipient of traumatic experiences and unsafe people, chances are our box gets filled with harmful traits about ourselves.

When someone is mean to us, and it affects us it's because what they saw in us is a trait we put in our box and is now a part of our identity. We would not get triggered if the underlying emotion it's bringing up within us wasn't already in our box. Introjection can impact a person's ability to regulate their emotions and express themselves. If a child grows up in an environment where their emotions are invalidated or dismissed, they may learn to suppress their feelings or express them in aggressive or inappropriate ways, which can contribute to anger issues in adulthood. Additionally, childhood stress can impact a person's self-esteem and sense of self-worth, leading to feelings of shame, guilt, or resentment that can fuel anger. For example, a person who experienced emotional abuse in childhood may

63

struggle with feelings of inadequacy or worthlessness, which can trigger intense anger when their sense of self is threatened.

Here are examples of internalizing labels:

-John graduated with honors and always did well in school and got accepted to all the top universities he applied to. Growing up, he never felt like his accomplishments were good enough for his dad. His father never validated his feelings or successes and always passed comments such as "don't act stupid" that made John doubt himself. One day he's having a few drinks in a bar and someone calls him stupid, and he yells at him in anger. John is very smart, but he owned someone else's projection of him because a part of him believed it to be true. He subconsciously had already felt like he was not smart enough and the person in the bar triggered that unhealed part of him.

-Peter graduated and got refused to 2 out of the three universities he applied to. His parents not only celebrated his achievements (small or big) but would always ask him "how do you feel about your grades?" which always gave him space to express his emotions authentically. The same situation happens in a bar where someone calls him stupid, but because he doesn't own those feelings, he disregards the comment and laughs it off.

You see what we put in our box can determine some of our adult triggers. When a person experiences stress, hurt, heartbreak, or even trauma in childhood, their developing brain can become hypersensitive to potential threats. This hypervigilance can be evident or oftentimes subconscious which in turn can manifest as anger, as the person may overreact to criticism, neglect, or other perceived "dangers".

It can be difficult to let go of resentment or anger towards people who have hurt us in the past. However, it is important to recognize that as adults, we have the power to take control of our own lives and behaviors, regardless of our upbringing or past experiences.

Here are some steps you can take to start the healing:

Recognize the impact of your upbringing. Acknowledge that your upbringing may have had an impact on your beliefs, behaviors, and thought patterns, but that it doesn't define who you are as a person. Understanding the root causes of your behaviors can help you take steps towards change.

Practice self-compassion. Instead of blaming yourself, your parents or anyone that hurt you for your behaviors, practice self-compassion and recognize that you are doing the best you can with the resources and knowledge you have at the moment. Treat yourself with kindness and understanding.

Take responsibility for your actions. While your upbringing may have had an impact on your behaviors, it is ultimately up to you to take responsibility for your actions and make changes in your life. Recognize that you have the power to change your thoughts, beliefs, and behaviors.

Seek help. Consider seeking the help of a mental health professional to work through any underlying issues related to your upbringing and to develop healthy coping mechanisms.

Forgive others if and when you are ready. Forgiveness is a powerful tool for letting go of resentment and anger. Forgiving people that hurt you does not mean condoning their actions or behaviors, but rather releasing yourself from the painful emotions that may be holding you back.

What we fail to realize is that everybody is self-projecting all the time. These subconscious feelings, thoughts, and opinions that others have about themselves are projected onto you when they do not have the ability to self-reflect. So oftentimes people will criticize us and say that we are a specific way when in fact they are reaching into their boxes and handing you their own thoughts, feelings, and expectations about themselves. We can choose whether we want to hold those opinions and put them in our boxes and now own those labels or we can reject them.

"Since the beginning of time, people have been trying to change the world so that they can be happy. This hasn't ever worked because it approaches the problem backward. What the work gives us is a way to change the projector — mind — rather than the projected. It's like when there's a piece of lint on a projector's lens. We think there's a flaw on the screen, and we try to change this person and that person, whomever the flaw appears on next. But it's futile to try to change the projected images. Once we realize where the lint is, we can clear the lens itself. This is the end of suffering, and the beginning of a little joy in paradise." Byron Katie

CHAPTER 5

SELF-PROJECTIONS AND TRIGGERS

An emotional trigger can come from an event, situation, or memory that sets off a strong emotional response in an individual. Triggers can vary widely in intensity and duration. For example, a person who has experienced trauma related to a particular sound, such as a glass breaking, may be triggered by that sound and experience intense fear or anxiety. Alternatively, a person who associates a particular smell with a happy memory, such as the scent of a specific perfume from their childhood, may feel joy or nostalgia when they encounter that scent later in life. Emotional triggers can also be related to values, beliefs, or identity. For example, someone who strongly identifies with a particular religious group may feel anger or frustration when they encounter information that contradicts their beliefs or values. It's important to note that emotional triggers are subjective and can vary from person to person based on their experiences and perceptions. What may be a trigger for one person may not be a trigger for another.

Triggers can also be associated with traumatic memories that are stored in our subconscious mind and have not been fully processed. These memories can be from recent or distant past experiences, and they can cause strong emotional reactions.

Some children are raised with the expectation that they should always be happy and well-behaved, or else they will face consequences such as reprimands, punishment, or even neglect. As they grow older, many of these individuals strive to maintain that same mentality, believing that if they remain positive and obedient, good things will happen, and they will continue to receive love and acceptance. However, in suppressing so-called "negative" emotions, these individuals are not truly releasing them but instead storing them in their subconscious.

The more emotions you push away, ignore, overcome, or as I say "suppress", the stronger the trigger will grow. Triggers don't usually come out when we are prepared, they are quick and unpredictable. These emotions can be powerful and can lead to a negative inner dialogue or self-criticism, which can in turn affect our self-esteem and how we feel about ourselves. For example, if a person has had a traumatic experience related to public speaking, they may feel triggered when asked to give a presentation. This could lead to feelings of anxiety, self-doubt, and negative self-talk, such as "I'm not good enough," or "I'm going to fail." These thoughts and feelings can then affect how they perceive themselves. Emotional triggers can also affect how you view others. When triggered, we may experience a strong emotional reaction that can color our perception of others, making it difficult to see them objectively. For example, if a person has a history of being bullied, they may feel triggered when they perceive someone as being aggressive or confrontational. This could lead to feelings of fear, anger, or resentment towards that person, even if the situation is not objectively threatening. It's important to recognize how our emotional triggers can affect our perceptions of others and to work towards addressing these biases. If triggers affect how we see ourselves and others, it will definitely affect what we are projecting onto others. So, to calm the intensity behind your triggers you need to validate and give attention to the feeling you've been hiding from yourself. Validating suppressed emotions can be a key step towards acknowledging and processing them. Here are some ways you can start healing triggers:

Practice mindfulness. This involves paying attention to the present moment without judgment. By becoming aware of your thoughts and feelings, you can begin to recognize and validate your emotions.

Write in a journal. Writing down your thoughts can help you identify and acknowledge suppressed emotions. You can also use journaling to explore the root causes of these emotions and work through them.

Talk to a trusted friend or specialist. Talking to someone who is non-judgmental and supportive can help you validate your emotions.

Engage in creative expression. Engaging in creative activities, such as dancing, art, or music, can provide an outlet and help you express and validate them in a safe and healthy way. Practice self-compassion. Recognize that it's okay to have those emotions and that you're not alone in experiencing them. Practicing empathy by being kind and understanding towards yourself. Becoming your best friend.

By working through our emotional triggers, we can develop a more balanced and compassionate view of others, which can improve our relationships and overall well-being. I have another practice for self-validation later in the book that is quite healing called Time Travel Reparenting. Let's do a little more self-reflection together before diving into that!

Social media question:

Anonymous: I believe this topic is triggering and gaslighting people

Answer: Gaslighting definition: to manipulate (someone) by psychological means into questioning their own sanity. An article by Psychology Today says: "Gaslighting is an insidious form of manipulation and psychological control. Victims of gaslighting are deliberately and systematically fed false *information that leads them to question what they know to be true, often about themselves. They may end up doubting their memory, their perception, and even their sanity. Over time, a gaslighter's manipulations can grow more complex and potent, making it increasingly difficult for the victim to see the truth."*

Here's were owning our self-projections and gaslighting are quite different. The answer is in the need for manipulation and control.

Psychology Today also said: "The term gaslighting comes from a 1938 play, Gas Light, and its film adaptation. Gaslighting can occur in personal or professional relationships, and victims are targeted at the core of their being: their sense of identity and self-worth. Manipulative people who engage in gaslighting do so to attain power over their victims."

The benefits of owning our self-projection are self-awareness and accountability, which refers to taking responsibility for one's actions or decisions and being answerable for their consequences. It involves acknowledging when one has done or said something hurtful and being willing to make amends or take corrective action. Accountability promotes honesty, trust, and personal growth, as it allows individuals to learn from their mistakes and make positive changes in their

72

behavior, unlike gaslighting which is used for control and manipulation.

I could argue that I, in the past, have been gaslit by someone who did not own their projections. An ex used to call me a manipulator pretty often during our relationship. I used to get confused about that and would ask him what made me a manipulator and he would try to convince me that asking him that question was me manipulating him. I eventually started to believe maybe he was right. I was owning his Absolved self-projection. Not owning his sh!t and forcing me to believe those things about me was a form of gaslighting. Remember self-empowerment versus control.

"Many of the faults you see in others, dear reader, are your own nature reflected in them." Rumi

PHYSICAL TRIGGERS

We have 5 basic senses (there are many more, but I'm addressing the basic ones).

Sight: colors, light, brightness, dimensions, depth, texture...
Taste: salty, sweet, bitter, sour, earthy, metals...
Touch: temperature, pressure, pain, itch, softness...
Sound: loud, vibrations, high, low...
Smell: fragrant, woody, minty, pungent, strong...

While we experience life through our 5 senses, we develop emotions connected to our experiences. We can feel all kinds of emotions when experiencing loud sounds, strong smells, or tastes.

Getting triggered from a sense can be a natural response. Let's use the sense of smell for example. There are several factors that can influence a person's sensitivity to smells, including genetic and biological factors. The sense of smell is a complex physiological process that involves specialized cells in the nose called olfactory receptors. These receptors are responsible for detecting and interpreting different smells. However, not all people have the same ability to perceive smells with the same intensity or clarity. For example, some people may have more olfactory receptors in their nose, which allows them to detect smells more easily. Other people may have fewer receptors, making it more difficult for them to detect certain smells. In some cases, getting triggered by a strong scent may be a learned behavior. For example, if you were raised in an environment where certain smells were associated with danger or negative experiences, your brain may have learned to associate those with fearful emotions or reactions. Moreover, certain biological factors can also influence a person's sensitivity to smells. For instance, hormonal changes, such as those that occur during pregnancy or menstruation. Medical conditions such as allergies, sinus infections, or neurological disorders can also impact a person's ability to detect and perceive different smells.

Our sense of smell is closely linked to the emotional centers of our brain, so strong odors can elicit strong emotional responses. Let's take my experience with my grandmother as an example. I had a very positive association with a certain type of candy (salted black licorice) that my grandmother always gave me when we would visit her as a child. I loved the taste and the memories it brought back of me spending time with her. Later in life, I found that same candy in a store and decided to try it again. As soon as I tasted it, I was flooded with happy memories of my grandmother and felt a strong emotional response of joy and nostalgia. In this case, the taste of the candy was triggering a positive emotional response based on my past experiences and memories.

What do self-projections have to do with physical triggers? Well, let me explain using an example of a question I got from a client. (To preserve her identity, let's call her Nancy). In our first session, she asked me: "I am very triggered by my husband's smell after returning from work. It makes me nauseated. I want him to shower because I can't stand the smell. I notice myself judging him and calling him stinky and gross. Am I self-projecting?"

Nancy initially thought she had to accept that certain smells made her angry and there was nothing that could change that. Her husband had to shower immediately after work or Nancy would get triggered and yell at him. She believed her anger was from the odor. After working on self-reflection, we were able to discover together that she was actually angry from feeling disrespected when her husband came home and sat on the couch beside her without showering after she had expressed to him several times how sick it made her feel. She felt a lack of compassion and consideration. Her boundary was not being respected. It's okay for Nancy to not like body odor or be sensitive to it, but before understanding her feelings she would react unconsciously with anger and shame her husband for a natural human issue.

If we have an emotionally charged response to people or events, we have to ask ourselves "Why?" We can't force others to own our triggers and take responsibility for how we feel, but we can control how we respond. In Nancy's case boundaries were needed. Boundaries or as I like to call them, "agreements" are healthy limits and guidelines we set for ourselves in our relationships with others. They involve communicating our needs, wants, and limits clearly and respectfully to others. They also require us to recognize and respect the boundaries of others. Agreements are saying "everyone's feelings matter." Nancy's husband had a long day and was too tired to shower but coming home smelly made the house smell which made Nancy nauseated. Compromises with her partner were needed in her case.

Now, where does the projection come into play here?

What were the adjectives Nancy initially used? "Stinky and gross". Has she ever felt stinky and gross and judged herself? Yes! She expressed to me that as a teen, she had experienced criticism from her mother when her hair was oily. Her mother often used the word "gross" when criticizing her. Nancy had stored that emotion in her subconscious mind and as she grew up, without realizing it, prided herself in having "the best" fresh clean hair all the time. Through our sessions, she realized how much money she was spending on weekly visits to the salon because of this hidden insecurity. She was able to find balance and set healthy boundaries for herself and her husband. Owning her projection unraveled layers of healing!

Another example was a client that constantly criticized his wife for her lack of cleanliness in the house. When we dug deep enough, the self-projection ended up being that the husband was jealous that his wife wasn't affected by the disorder and remained happy even when the house was messy. It never affected her inner peace, and it would for him. Compromises and agreements were needed in the relationship. Once we uncovered the self-projection, he noticed his relationship changed for the better! Not just with his wife but with himself.

You see, it's never about fixing ourselves. With self-awareness, we can effectively communicate our needs to those close to us. When we don't know our triggers, we can lash out at others and verbalize our self-projections which in turn can hurt those around us. We cannot assume others should know what we need when we're not even clear on what we need ourselves! I will be giving tools later on in the book on how to set healthy agreements with those close to us.

SELF-PROJECTION AND ABUSE

Now let's address the most common question I get. If I see a narcissist, does that make me one? Let's self-reflect and get uncomfortable.

If a trained professional has diagnosed an individual with narcissistic personality disorder following an assessment, then it is a fact that the person can be referred to as a narcissist. This analysis was not made with an emotional charge behind it, it was determined with verifiable evidence. It is also a fact that undiagnosed narcissism is common, and NPD can be difficult to identify, as individuals with this condition may not seek help or may be reluctant to acknowledge that they have a problem. They may also be skilled at hiding their true nature and present a charming and likable persona to the outside world. We discussed earlier facts versus self-projections. If you came to a conclusion without assumption and emotion and remain objective, it may be possible that you correctly identified the behavior of an undiagnosed narcissist. The fact is narcissistic personality disorder is a mental health condition that can be characterized by a grandiose sense of self-importance, a lack of empathy for others, a need for excessive admiration, and a tendency to exploit and manipulate others for personal gain.

If you're still not sure if you're self-projecting or not, let's work on this some more while using what we've learned so far.

If you don't relate to labeling narcissists, perhaps try this exercise with another projected "negative" opinion you may have about someone, for instance a manipulator or liar.

Grab a paper and a pen and jot down your answers: Think of someone you believe is _____.

What is the definition of a _____ ?

Self-reflection questions:

What are my Emotional self-projections? What positive or negative emotions arise in me when I recognize a _____? What do I feel about the _____? (adjective)
Ex: I am intolerant to narcissists (At times, am I intolerant towards myself?)

Am I Presumption self-projecting? What do I believe others feel about the _____? Do I believe everyone thinks that this individual is a _____? Am I assuming or are there verifiable facts?

Am I Knowledge self-projecting? Do I feel like the _____ should know better? Should they know what

I know? Do I feel _____ people should know what to do when they are tempted to act a certain way?

Am I Absolved self-projecting? Are there logical and verifiable facts when I am labeling that person? If I am assuming without facts, do I recognize similar behavior in me? Have I now or have I been or acted like a _____?

After self-reflection, you may discover that:

1- You felt an Emotional self-projection about them because you've felt and recognized those emotions in you. (In this case, the time travel reparenting technique I will show you, later on, can help ease the hurt.)

2. You correctly recognized the behavior in others with facts.

3- You may have Absolved self-projected this behavior onto others because you have been or may still be acting this way.

The action related to the feeling that you're having does not have to be the same as what the other person is doing. What I mean by that, is if your opinion of a person for example is that they run fast, it doesn't have to mean that you run fast. It can simply mean that "fast" is something that you may feel about yourself (a fast worker or a fast eater for example). If you think some people are "detestable" because they

81

cheated. Your self-projected emotion of feeling detestable doesn't necessarily have to come from cheating.

*If you suspect that you or someone you know may be struggling with abusive or narcissistic traits or behaviors, it is important to seek the help of a mental health.

A trained specialist can help identify underlying issues and work with the individual to develop strategies for managing their symptoms and improving their relationships and overall quality of life.

Being online I've noticed a rise in the word toxic. Many people are using these words when they are hurt by someone else's actions and words or lack of. It is important when doing reflection work, we become mindful of our words towards ourselves and others.

"Projections are, so to speak, the instruments of perception which adapt the subject to the world."

Carl Jung

Let's talk about a common self-projection: prejudiced.

Prejudice refers to a preconceived opinion or attitude towards a person or a group of people that is not based on reason or actual experience. Prejudice often involves negative feelings or beliefs about a particular group of people, such as stereotypes or generalizations, and may lead to discrimination or unfair treatment based on those preconceptions.

If this definition doesn't resonate with you, break down the meaning of what that word means to you. If you've assumed this about others, creating perhaps a generalization without having facts, they could be coming from a judgment that was formed from an opinion. Generalization can also lead to oversimplification, or biased thinking, especially when it is based on incomplete or inaccurate information. If you feel like most people are prejudiced, I urge you to find out in what aspects of your life may this adjective be present. Prejudiced can be based on various factors:

Racism: Prejudiced based on a person's race or ethnicity, often involving negative stereotypes and discriminatory attitudes towards individuals who belong to certain racial or ethnic groups.

Sexism: Prejudiced based on a person's gender, often involving negative stereotypes and discriminatory attitudes

Homophobia: Prejudiced based on a person's sexual orientation, often involving negative stereotypes and discriminatory attitudes towards individuals who identify as LGBTQ+.

Ageism: Prejudiced based on a person's age, often involving negative stereotypes and discriminatory attitudes towards individuals who are younger or older than a certain age.

Ableism: Prejudiced based on a person's physical or mental abilities, often involving negative stereotypes and discriminatory attitudes towards individuals who have disabilities.

Spiritual Prejudiced: based on a person's religious or spiritual beliefs or affiliation, often involving negative stereotypes and discriminatory attitudes towards individuals who belong to certain religions or hold certain beliefs.

Prejudiced based on socioeconomic status: Involves negative attitudes or stereotypes towards individuals or groups based on their social and economic background. This type of prejudice can be based on assumptions about a person's education, income, occupation, or other aspects of their social status. For example, a person may be prejudiced against those who are living in poverty, assuming that they are lazy or uneducated, without considering the systemic and structural barriers that may have contributed to their situation. Alternatively, a person may be prejudiced against those who are wealthy, assuming that they are entitled or morally corrupt, without recognizing that not all wealthy individuals have equal access to opportunities and resources.

If you often recognize prejudiced people, what are you self-projecting? Let's ask ourselves some questions:

Emotional self-projection: Are you prejudiced toward yourself? Review the types and ask yourself if you have ever criticized yourself.

Presumption self-projection: Are you assuming many people feel the same way you do? When people are feeling the same, does that bring you validation? If so, what makes you feel unworthy when people disagree?

Knowledge self-projection: Do you feel like everyone should know what you know? Do you feel triggered when someone doesn't share your knowledge?

Absolved self-projection: Are you prejudiced toward others? Review the types. If so, where does that feeling come from and how could you grow compassion for others and yourself?

When we find true happiness within ourselves, we no longer feel the need to criticize or judge others.

ARE WE TO BLAME FOR OUR PAST

Remember, it is never about being perfect because human perfection is unattainable. The key here is simply to be aware. When you're triggered by someone and you find yourself getting emotional or judgmental and start taking out your frustration on someone else, it is important to stop for a moment and ask yourself: first, where is this coming from? Second: what in me feels this way? And third, what am I self-projecting? If we practice this regularly, the need for blame fades away and accountability replaces it. Accepting that we all have our issues, whether they stemmed from our past, ancestral trauma, or even as some believe "past life trauma," you are actively stopping the cycle by saying I own all my feelings and emotions.

I often get the question, "but Tanya? Am I to blame for being verbally or physically abused? Am I to blame for getting yelled at or being lied to? Do I have to take responsibility for how people treat me?" I need to emphasize here you are NOT responsible for other people's words, actions, and emotions. We cannot control how people feel and what they do. Self-projections have nothing to do with how people treat you. It is about the emotional opinion that you are projecting onto others. The responsibility for abusive behavior lies with the abuser. No one deserves to be mistreated. You have the right to set boundaries and communicate your needs calmly and respectfully, and if someone continues to yell or behave inappropriately, it may be necessary to remove yourself from the situation and seek support from others. If someone is abusing you or someone else, the action was abusive. That is simply a fact. Please don't blame yourself because of someone else's actions towards you.

There's a fine line between blaming ourselves and taking accountability. Blame has the intention of shame behind it without a solution.

In the case of Absolved-Self-Projections, when we blame others for our own actions, such as yelling, lying, or being abusive, we are essentially justifying our behavior by absolving ourselves and shifting the blame and guilt onto the other person. On the other hand, when we blame ourselves for being on the receiving end of such negative behavior, we are justifying the other person's actions and placing the guilt and blame on ourselves. True accountability means taking responsibility for our actions and looking for a solution, rather than placing blame.

As Sadhguru explains, responsibility is about our "ability to respond" to people and situations in each moment, choosing how, what, and when we want to respond. While we cannot control how others treat us, we do have control over how we treat ourselves. Owning our own thoughts and behaviors is not about blaming or victim-shaming, but rather about empowering ourselves, increasing our self-awareness, and finding a deeper sense of inner peace.

Question from social media:

Blue Freddo: *How does someone with a trauma project compare to someone without trauma?*

Answer: *Trauma can be caused by extreme events or many small ones. It's not what we live but how our brain processes that pain and hurt. Some people go through such incredibly painful traumatic events but turn out to be gentle and kind, and some people live a few hurtful events but experience more suffering. This is why we cannot compare painful events. I remember a moment in my life when I was in the hospital on life support. I had just gotten a kidney transplant, but the kidney hadn't started working yet. I had a 1-year-old baby at home, and I was eager to get better so I could get back to her. A friend came to visit me during this time. She was telling me about her life, complaining how hard it was and that "God" must hate her because she had so much homework and her parents were on her case. At that moment I couldn't understand how she could tell me this while I had a tube in my neck, but it became clear to me later on that she suffered with anxiety. Although I was physically in pain, my mind was thinking of my beautiful baby girl, and I was not feeling as* *"bad" emotionally as my friend. This is why we can't compare events and trauma. As I mentioned earlier on, we perceive life differently with our senses. It's not about what we went through, it's how we were able to process it. The more awareness and acceptance of emotions, the softer the response and the calmer the triggers.*

CHAPTER 6

PROJECTIONS CAN'T TELL TIME

Our emotional mind doesn't fully grasp the concept of time.

Take our brain for instance. It consists of about 86 billion neurons, interconnected by around 100 trillion synapses. It is a challenge to comprehend the intricacies of the functioning of these cells, and even more so to comprehend how they collaborate to form our sensory systems, behavior, and emotions. Our brain is constantly processing sensory information and creating a subjective experience of time. Our memories of the past are stored in different parts of our brain, while our perceptions of the present are processed by our sensory organs and interpreted by our brain in real-time. Our mind also anticipates the future based on our past experiences and our expectations. Our past, present, and future are intimately linked by our memories.

I would like you to keep this in mind when thinking about self-projections. Our emotions can get confused by our past, present, and future, and so can our self-projections. What I mean by that is sometimes when you are projecting a feeling, it may be an emotion you used to feel often but it is presently dormant within you.

In the past, I used to judge people who were verbally aggressive. Over time I realized that I was also guilty of being verbally aggressive when someone close to me hurt me. I was Absolved self-projecting. I would justify my behavior by telling myself that I was simply defending myself. When someone triggered me, I would respond by raising my voice. I now understand that my intense reactions were not a true reflection of who I was as a person. Rather, they were the result of a deeply wounded child within me who was trying to protect herself. I was so hurt and did not know how to express my emotions or set boundaries, which resulted in me tolerating a lot of mistreatments from others.

Over the years I became increasingly aware of my triggers and have learned to communicate my needs in a healthier way. I am no longer verbally aggressive and have a deeper understanding and empathy for those who struggle with similar issues. Once I owned this projection, I was able to give a lot of love to that hurt child within me. Over time I learned to not only heal that part but find a steady balance within my emotions. I learned I cannot control others, I can only control how I respond. Although this is in my past, in the present time, I can still recognize it in others because it was, and always will be a part of me. What used to be "loud and aggressive" is now "firm and assertive." I have not changed, I just shifted my awareness. When I do recognize it in others now, I have two choices: Judge them or self-reflect and have compassion. I will always have that strong-willed side but because I have love for it, it doesn't have power over me anymore. I can use that assertiveness in circumstances where it is needed. For example, a few years ago my daughter was getting bullied by a bus driver at her school. I approached him and he denied everything even knowing we had recordings proving his behavior. I used my firm, assured voice, and approached the situation calmly with the principal of the school. My bold approach was taken seriously, and they immediately took action. A camera was placed on the bus and the driver was given a warning. He ultimately changed his approach to how he spoke to the children. We have the choice to blame or to look within. I have a vision of a kinder, more compassionate, loving world where we can look internally and learn the healing power of owning our sh!t.

The distinction between past, present, and future is only a stubbornly persistent illusion."
Albert Einstein

THE FLAWED MIND

We have an organizing network in our brain called the reticular activating system that filters out information that contradicts our beliefs. The R.A.S. is a complex network of neurons located in the brainstem. It acts as a filter that sorts and prioritizes incoming sensory information, allowing only the most important signals to reach the brain's higher centers. It receives input from various sensory systems, including visual, auditory, somatosensory (touch), and emotional inputs, and integrates this information to determine whether it is relevant or not. It then sends signals to the thalamus and other brain structures, activating or inhibiting them, depending on the significance of the incoming stimuli. Basically, our brain will push to the forefront what it deems as important.

This filter can be influenced by our beliefs and biases. For instance, if I believe that my friend is frequently angry, I may overlook the times when she's happy and smiling, as my brain tends to notice and remember information that confirms my beliefs. Similarly, our brains tend to highlight the things we value and pay less attention to the rest, just like when we buy a new car and start seeing it everywhere. Again, we cannot control the R.A.S. but when we become aware that it exists, we can understand that we may not be seeing the whole picture when we create opinions and assumptions about others. When we expand our awareness, we become more attuned to the experiences of others, which can lead to increased empathy, better communication, and stronger relationships.

There's this great story that I heard from Spidey, the behavioral analysis therapist and mentalist on YouTube. Spidey talks about numerous studies that have shown that providing individuals with false evidence can lead them to create false memories. One notable study in this field is Kimberly Wade's "A Picture is Worth 1000 Lies," in which individuals were shown a photoshopped image of themselves in a hot air balloon as a child, despite never having been on one before. Shockingly, 50% of participants subsequently "remembered" the event and even recalled details about their experience, despite it being entirely fabricated. Our memory is inherently flawed, prioritizing practicality over accuracy and becoming even more malleable when emotions and imagination are involved. As a result, we may incorporate memories from unrelated events or even entirely fabricate them while feeling certain that they are genuine. Being mindful of our Reticular Activating System is crucial as it enables us to rely on our self-projections rather than making flawed assumptions about others. Recognizing the limitations of our own minds helps us develop a better understanding of ourselves.

THE LANGUAGE OF ABSOLUTES

Oftentimes when we are upset about someone else's words and actions or lack of, we will use words like ALWAYS and NEVER.

Using "always" and "never" in certain contexts can be problematic because they are absolute terms that imply that something is true or false 100% of the time, which is often not the case. For example, saying "You always forget to do your homework" or "You never listen to me" may not accurately reflect the reality of the situation, and can come across as overly critical or accusatory. It's important to use language that accurately reflects the situation and to avoid making sweeping generalizations based on limited or incomplete information. Instead of using "always" and "never", it may be more helpful to use more nuanced language that acknowledges the complexities of the situation. I will use an example of how these words can be used when we are unaware of our self-projections.

I got a comment on a self-projection video I posted that said: *"My mother-in-law lies all the time and my sister-in-law, and I judge her. I never lie so I am not self-projecting."*

Let's break this down. *"My mother-in-law lies ALL THE TIME* (always)." This means no sentence that has ever come out of her mouth is truthful. This can be an example of confirmation bias. Her mother-in-law may often be telling truthful stories, but her brain may not remember those times. Her reticular activating system may filter out the times she is honest. If she does have verifiable evidence of her mother-in-law lying often and she was simply exaggerating, then she could become aware of the words she used and evaluate her comment. If someone frequently exaggerates the way people act or what they say, people may start to doubt the truthfulness of their claims, which can harm their reputation and credibility. It can lead to misunderstandings and hurt feelings, which can damage relationships with others. When someone exaggerates the severity of a situation, it can make it difficult to find practical solutions to problems. It can cause unnecessary stress and can prevent them from accurately assessing and addressing issues in their life.

In the next part, she says:

"My sister-in-law and I judge her." -Adding a person to confirm what we believe about someone is often used to get validation and to prove that what we believe is a fact. We often use this technique because we were not taught at a young age to validate ourselves. That in of itself is a projected emotion coming from her as she clearly said "I" judge her.

Become aware when you hear yourself using strong affirming words like always and never or synonyms. Moreover, when we are experiencing high intensities of emotions such as anger or happiness, studies have shown that we tend to distort our memories during those moments.

As the wonderful Maya Angelou once said: *"I've learned that people will forget what you said, people will forget what you did, but people will never forget how you made them feel."*

So, if human memory is prone to error and our reticular activating system is continuously making us forget certain behaviors of other people, wouldn't you think our feelings about others are correlated with a part of ourselves that we are projecting onto them? Something to think about.

"If you surrender to uncertainty, nothing goes wrong." Deepak Chopra

WHAT AM I PROJECTING IN THE WORLD

The world has always been filled with love, peace, and serenity but also chaos, power, and control. Because we have access to infinite amounts of information at our fingertips, there is a growing awareness among people regarding the persistent societal issues that have been ignored or gone unnoticed for too long.

Those who know me, know I love investigating conspiracies. I love to live in the "maybe" but here's why and how I don't let myself get sucked into the "new age matrix awakening" as I like to call it. This interpretation of the "Matrix" suggests that certain events or circumstances indicate the involvement of a covert and potentially harmful group or organization in shaping the course of society. "Awakening" to some means, becoming aware of a wide range of topics, such as government cover-ups, secret societies, or paranormal phenomena. This group of people may distrust or reject mainstream sources of information, instead relying on alternative sources, and may exhibit a high degree of skepticism toward official accounts of events such as the moon landing, what happened on 9/11, or towards vaccines.

My version of the term "Matrix" is the idea that there is a larger, hidden reality beyond the physical world we see and experience in our everyday lives. A belief that we are all interconnected and that there is a collective consciousness and energy field that we are all a part of. Accepting the possibility that the physical world is an illusion created by us, and that with awareness we can embrace the physical and spiritual world while feeling the love within us. I have comfort in uncertainty. I understand why many people believe in the first interpretation, but I've been there and when you get caught up in anger and fear, over time that can become what you self-project onto the world, which in turn separates you from love.

Would you like to know what you are projecting on a larger scale? What do you feel about what is happening in the world right now? Could that be a reflection of you? Let's find out.

Subject: *World*

2 positive ways to describe it (adjectives):

2 negative ways to describe it (adjectives):

Facts: what has been proven (verifiable information, without emotion):

Here are some examples of questions you can self-reflect on: If you see division in the world: Are you divided within yourself? Think of a moment when you were self-critical. Do you sometimes wish you were living another person's experiences? For example, someone lacking financial stability wishes they were born into a wealthy family.

If you see hate in the world: What do you hate about yourself? Do you wish to change something about yourself? What makes you hate that part of you?

If you can't answer these questions, then dive deeper! This exercise may feel uncomfortable, but the idea here is not to fix anything, just to become aware of something you may have been suppressing within yourself. If the world makes us angry, unless we are actively infiltrated into the system and trying to make a change from within the organizations, all we are doing is complaining. If we don't have the means to change the system, perhaps the change we need to see is the change within our thoughts.

"The world as we have created it is a process of our thinking. It cannot be changed without changing our thinking." Albert Einstein

CHAPTER 7

INTUITION OR PROJECTION

To differentiate between intuition and self-projections, let's begin by discussing intuition.

Intuition is a sense that operates without rational thought. It can be difficult to distinguish intuition from an intrusive thought because when we have an intuitive feeling, we tend to try and rationalize it with our conscious mind. Intuition is instinctive and can be felt throughout the body without any emotion or explanation attached to it. Intuition has no intention, judgment, or emotion associated with it; it is simply a "sense of knowing."

In the spiritual community, it is believed that "Intuition is the way the subconscious mind communicates with the conscious mind." I somewhat disagree. I believe intuition goes beyond the subconscious mind and it is connected with our consciousness (soul or spirit, whatever you want to call it!) The word "consciousness" is derived from the Latin word "conscientia," which means "knowledge within oneself" or "with knowledge." The field of consciousness study is vast and expansive, making it challenging to assign its theory to any particular individual or group, given the continuous evolution of research over time. Renowned figures who have contributed to this field include philosophers such as René Descartes, Immanuel Kant, and John Locke, as well as psychologists like Sigmund Freud and Carl Jung, and physicists such as Albert Einstein and Erwin Schrödinger in the 20th century. In recent years, neuroscientists such as Christof Koch, Giulio Tononi, and David Chalmers have made significant contributions to the study of consciousness but not much has been said to the public yet. We know it exists, but we still have so many unanswered questions about "the energy that makes our body alive."

I believe that intuition is a sort of communication or connection between our consciousness and our subconscious. Like a form of transmission. Intuition doesn't cause pain in the body and doesn't come with any intrusive thoughts. Whether it's to protect us, protect others, or guide us, it is instinctual. Picture it like a phone call. Your consciousness is calling your body. You don't know who's calling or why, you just pick up.

If you don't listen to your intuition, that's when your conscious mind will try to rationalize this and give you that "gut pain" feeling. You'll start using your subconscious memories, past experiences, and self-projections to evaluate the situation. This is when your intrusive thoughts can cloud your mind.

While intuition can be a useful tool for making quick decisions, it is also subject to biases and errors. It may not always be reliable or accurate because many people confuse intuition with intrusive thoughts. We confuse these two because when our thoughts turn out to be right, we believe it was our intuition! Assumptions can sometimes turn out to be right, but it doesn't mean you weren't still projecting a feeling.

If you end up being right about an "intrusive thought" and feel validated that's ok but remember that growth comes from self-awareness. Being "right" may feel good temporarily however it can over time become problematic. It leads to an inability to listen to others while considering alternative perspectives.

Having a strong sense of confidence in one's intuition can be a positive attribute in certain situations, such as when making important decisions or standing up for oneself. However, it's important to balance that confidence with openness to feedback, willingness to learn from others, and a recognition that one's perspective may not always be accurate or complete.

"Intuition is the whisper of the soul."
J. Krishnamurti

THE BOOMERANG

Have you ever encountered a situation where you find it difficult to stop thinking about someone, such as an ex, a family member, or a friend who not in your life? If you're actively engaged in the process of moving on from them, I have personally employed a technique I call "boomerang redirecting," which I have successfully utilized with both myself and my clients over the years. This technique that I will be showing you, aids in letting go of someone.

I am frequently asked about the energetic bonds that exist between individuals. When people struggle to break free from persistent thoughts about someone, they often presume that there must be a potent force linking them together. Have you ever been convinced that your attachment to someone was due to a powerful energetic or spiritual bond? Your intuition may have suggested that there may have been a deeper connection between you and the other person. If you assume an energetic or spiritual connection with someone without knowing factually if the feeling is mutual, it is important to consider whether these thoughts are beneficial for you. If the person you're thinking about is not in your life or not reaching out to you and you're experiencing pain from this lack of contact, it is possible that your intuition is not based on fact but rather from an Absolved self-projection of your own desires. While it may be true that unexplainable connections can occur between certain people, if you are the only one experiencing this feeling, it belongs solely to you. It is possible that your subconscious mind is influencing these thoughts and feelings associated with limerence. It is crucial to differentiate between intuition and self-projection when it comes to our emotions about others. Assuming a deep connection with someone based purely on intuition, without any factual basis, over time can create repetitive thought patterns. These patterns can turn into habits. A habit is a behavior that we repeat regularly, and it often occurs unconsciously. Habits can be formed intentionally or unintentionally, and they can become deeply ingrained and automatic over time, making them challenging to break or change. So, if it's hard to stop thinking of someone, it may be an unconscious habit. Projecting our emotions onto others, presuming the feeling is reciprocated, can drain our energy and lead to emotional distress, anxiety, or sadness.

Let's try the boomerang redirecting process together. To illustrate, picture your thoughts and emotions like a frisbee. Instead of throwing your thoughts "your frisbee" at the person you are fixated on, hoping they will return the energy, I suggest you imagine your thoughts and emotions as a boomerang. When you catch yourself thinking about someone, you could instead acknowledge and validate your feelings, (saying things like: My feelings matter, I matter.)

Then imagine the energy you have been directing towards them returning back to you like a boomerang.

I often utilize the "boomerang" exercise to help clients shift their focus away from the other person and turn their attention towards themselves. If you are struggling with constantly thinking of someone who isn't in your life, try this: Tell yourself what you want to tell the other person, such as how much you miss or love them, or anything else that you feel you need to express. You can even text yourself, reminding yourself that you deserve the energy you have been giving to the other person. This shift in energy can help you let go of unrequited thought patterns that involve other people, which may be causing you emotional distress or pain. If you find yourself fixating on someone, it is essential to consider the facts before making assumptions about a connection with them. You can use the boomerang exercise to redirect your thoughts and emotions toward yourself, which can help break the habit of projecting your feelings onto others. If you find yourself unable to move on from a past relationship, with your thoughts and emotions fixated on that person, and you desire to let go but are unsure how to do so, this technique can be immensely helpful as well.

In chapter 9, I have an exercise that can assist you in redirecting your thoughts and emotions. If you find that your belief in your own assumptions is hindering your ability to learn and grow, it may be worth exploring why you feel this way and work on developing more flexibility in your thinking. Awareness of self is what separates opinions and assumptions from growth.

Next time you feel like your intuition is present, ask yourself:

1. Am I assuming or stating facts?
2. Am I feeling discomfort from an intrusive thought, or does this feel calm?
3. Did I feel reactive or was I able to respond lovingly?

Intuition   Intrusive Thoughts

Calm	Hectic, Fear Inducing
Solves Problems	Creates Problems
Quiet	Loud
Unpredictable	Triggered By the Past
Loving	Fearful
Awareness, Calm Response	No Awareness, Reactive
No Worry	Worry
No pain	Pain, Discomfort

ATTRACTING VS ALLOWING

The Law of Attraction is constant and suggests that our thoughts and beliefs can influence our experiences and reality. Many people have different theories when it comes to the L.O.A. Some believe *"like attracts like"*, meaning when we are positive, we attract positive experiences and people into our lives, while negative thoughts and beliefs will attract negative experiences and people. Some believe that *"we attract what we believe"* which means, whatever we believe to our core is what will manifest in our lives. In this theory, if you believe you can manifest good stuff even when you're negative then you can. Others believe the law of attraction is *"we attract who we are,"* which is anything and everything, meaning, we are constant magnets, one consciousness experiencing itself. The belief that we're pure potential energy here to simply experience contrast is the concept that resonates most with me. This principle is based on the idea that everything in the universe is made up of energy, including our thoughts and emotions. No energy is good or bad, it just is. As I stated at the beginning of this book, I once held the belief that I needed to maintain a positive mindset at all times to prevent negative situations and people from entering my life. However, this constant effort to manage my negative thoughts and outcomes proved to be draining because despite my best efforts to maintain a positive outlook, I still encountered painful outcomes. It wasn't until I broadened my beliefs and embraced the concept of duality that I discovered inner peace. I realized that while I couldn't always control who I attracted, I had the power to decide who I allowed into my life. Rather than constantly questioning what and why I'm attracting certain things, I focus on why and what I allow. By putting my energy towards loving intentions, I can navigate my life with greater ease and manifest experiences that align with those intentions. Understanding what we allow can be empowering. As young children, we especially have no control over how people treat us and sadly we can be subject to other people's toxic behavior and abuse.

A family friend had suffered horrible abuse from their parents. Unimaginable things happened in this child's life. At the age of 10 this child was rescued from this abusive family and with a lot of love, support, and therapy, they turned their life around. This child could grow up to believe that the world is a dangerous and abusive place because of their past, or they can grow up thinking that the world is filled with love and support because they got rescued and got help. We cannot control what has happened to us, but we can control how we process it. As adults, we can take accountability for how we feel. We can grow and learn to set healthy boundaries and realize that our feelings matter, and we matter. Or we can suppress everything that has happened to us and project it onto others, blaming everyone around us for our subconscious unhappiness. Whichever path you take is up to you. We can choose to take responsibility for what we allow in our day-to-day life as adults by asking ourselves why do I allow this? Why is this okay for me?

When we find out why, we can then say, "now what?" Remember "why" should be asked to enter awareness and not to shame ourselves. Kids are too young and defenseless to have the ability to "allow" or not, but as adults we do, at some level, have the capability of setting emotional and physical boundaries.

*PLEASE NOTE: I am speaking about people in our day-to-day life. I am not addressing violent moments of attack and abuse. We cannot put those in the same category. WE ARE NEVER RESPONSIBLE FOR BEING ATTACKED or abused, WE DIDN'T ALLOW THEM TO ATTACK or abuse us.

By engaging in self-reflection, we can uncover and examine these patterns and beliefs, and become more conscious of the thoughts and emotions that may be blocking our growth. In other words, owning our projections can help us identify and change the limiting beliefs that may be holding us back from achieving our goals, and replace them with empowering beliefs that are aligned with our desires. Giving your subconscious hurt feeling a lot of love and validation can help you radiate more love!

Question from social media.

Gina: I have cancer and people tell me different things: either I attracted it, it's my soul contract or it's my karma. Self-projecting is about accountability so do I have to own this? *Answer:* What people are saying to you could be a fear coming from them and they are projecting that fear onto you. What they think is "fact" is simply a belief. I do believe finding a balance within our emotions can help heal our physical body to a certain degree. While we are suffering from a cold for example, what thoughts and emotions do we allow our mind to dwell on? I have physically suffered but over time I realized my emotional suffering always made it worse. I strongly believe we don't attract what makes us sick, but we can choose the path we take while healing. Pain is information. If we validate and listen to it instead of shaming, blaming, or ignoring it, the healing process, however long it takes, can be much more pleasant. Picking at a wound versus caring for it. A level of surrendering to the unknown can be peaceful. If others are projecting an emotion or belief onto you, remember what I said in chapter 8 about labels. I'm aware many people believe we are responsible for our sick bodies but if that's the case, does blaming it on yourself, karma or soul contracts heal the disease? We all have the same fate so why use this time on Earth to shame each other? Let's start with compassion, the highest form of love.

THE ABSENCE OF PROJECTIONS

When we disagree with others who judge people or situations, it may be because we lack the ability to project a mental movie if the scene is not stored in our subconscious. To illustrate, throughout the years, I formed various types of friendships; some were effortless, while others demanded more time and energy. While on my journey of healing, I began to discover my self-worth. For a long time, I did not believe that I had any importance or value on this planet. I believed that the emotions of others always held greater weight than mine. Other people's beliefs, opinions, and financial statuses carried more significance than my own. I had a beauty and wellness spa for several years and was committed to providing excellent services at a low cost. My intention was to help others, and it brought me satisfaction. However, as a single mother who underwent six surgeries, I would have benefited from a higher income and less financial pressure. Despite feeling exhausted after lengthy workdays, I continued to persevere because my clients' contentment in saving money held greater importance to me than my personal desire to earn more. I frequently put my feelings aside to please others. Some friends in my life warned me about certain people and advised me to be cautious of self-serving individuals, but I did not believe them. I was unable to recognize the selfish aspects of others because I did not possess that aspect myself.

As time passed, putting my feelings aside, led to feelings of resentment within me. For instance, if I were to fall ill and had to cancel an appointment, and my client would show resistance or frustration, I would immediately feel disrespected and blocked them. Similarly, if a friend failed to check up on me when I was unwell, considering all the help I had given them in the past, I would cut them off completely. I was naive to the fact that these were the unhealthy consequences of not expressing my boundaries. It was around then that I started calling people selfish for disrespecting me, not realizing I was self-projecting 2 emotions.

I was Absolved self-projecting "selfish": I had started to become selfish by lacking consideration for their feelings when I cut them off. I absolve myself by saying they deserved it because they were being selfish. I couldn't project that feeling prior to me acting unconsciously selfish.

I was also Emotional self-projecting "feeling disrespected": I was calling them disrespectful when in fact I wasn't respecting myself enough to set boundaries when I was sick.

Unknowingly, I was nurturing anger within myself, which eventually caused me to cut off a person I deeply cared about. This event forced me to embark on a self-reflection journey to understand why I was reacting in such a manner. I discovered that the resentment I felt was not directed towards those around me but towards myself. I realized that I hadn't considered setting healthy boundaries with anyone in my life, and my tendency to keep giving until I couldn't give anymore was the root cause of my problem. I asked myself some questions and realized that I was cutting people out of my life because I felt disrespected, but I knew it was not productive to blame them. So, I tried to understand why I felt that way and concluded that it was because I tended to give too much without feeling valued in return. It dawned on me that I was self-projecting these feelings onto others instead of empowering myself. Therefore, I decided to take ownership of my projections and found ways to respect and value myself, such as setting healthy limits, practicing self-worth affirmations, and showing compassion for myself. Ultimately, I learned to balance giving and receiving, which brought me more inner peace and fulfillment. Over time, I have learned how crucial healthy boundaries are when it comes to recognizing our own self-value.

CHAPTER 8

BOUNDARIES / AGREEMENTS

I like to call healthy boundaries, agreements. Because this is a sensitive and sometimes confusing topic for many, I chose to use a softer word with the same meaning. Healthy "agreements" are the limits we set for ourselves in relationships and interactions with others to empower and protect our physical, emotional, and spiritual well-being. These boundaries help us establish a sense of self-value, self-respect, and self-care, and they allow us to maintain healthy and fulfilling relationships with others. They can strengthen healthy relationships and help us filter through the ones that may not be good for us.

Agreements with others can be: Speaking up when someone violates our personal space. Setting limits on the amount of time we spend with people. Being honest about our feelings and needs with others, while respecting their feelings and needs as well. Agreements with ourselves can be: Taking care of our physical and emotional health by prioritizing sleep, exercise, healthy eating, and self-care activities.

Oftentimes when we're doing inner work and self-reflection we may tend to forget about healthy agreements. We're growing compassion and empathy for ourselves and others, so we are more lenient when it comes to other people's words and actions when they make us uncomfortable.

Feeling a little guilty when setting a boundary is normal, especially if you're not used to having rules for yourself. It also means you have compassion. When you set agreements, you're saying: my feelings matter, I matter. If you don't set boundaries you're unconsciously saying "Their feelings matter more than mine" when actually, everybody's feelings matter! If you're not sure how to set agreements, know that all of humanity is new at this so please don't shame yourself if you are unsure of how to start.

If you're struggling to set agreements altogether, you may find yourself ignoring certain behaviors that can be disrespectful or even harmful. If we are in a relationship where we ignore red flags at the beginning and accept verbal and physical abuse, we are not to blame for their words and actions, but we do play a part by staying in that environment. We are allowing over-and-over behavior that is hurtful and even dangerous.

There are several reasons why ignoring red flags can be easier for some than setting healthy boundaries:

-Fear of rejection or abandonment. When you set boundaries, you're essentially telling someone that you have limits and that they can't cross them. This can be scary because you might worry that the other person will reject you or abandon the relationship altogether.

-Feeling guilt or obligation. You might feel guilty or obligated to say yes to someone's request or to put their needs before your own. This can make it difficult to set agreements because you don't want to disappoint or upset the other person.

-Lacking confidence. Setting boundaries requires assertiveness, which is the ability to express your thoughts and feelings in a clear, confident, and respectful way. If you struggle with assertiveness, it can be challenging to set agreements without feeling rude or confrontational.

-Fear of disagreements. Setting boundaries can sometimes lead to conflict, which can be uncomfortable or scary for some people. This fear can make it hard to speak up and assert your needs. In addition, in some cultures or societies, setting boundaries may not be encouraged or may even be seen as disrespectful. This can make it challenging to set boundaries without feeling like you're going against the norm. When someone you care about is setting a boundary with you it's because they want to keep the relationship, they have with you all while feeling like their feelings matter. It is not an attempt to hurt you. It's important to remember that setting boundaries is a skill that can be learned and practiced. Becoming aware is the first step.

If you're in a situation where you feel like you can't set agreements, it's important to seek support from a friend or a healthcare provider who can help you take the necessary steps to ensure your safety.

NEGOTIABLE AND NON-NEGOTIABLES

We all have needs and wants with ourselves and others. Wouldn't it be great if we didn't have to tell anyone what we need, and they would simply just know? Unfortunately, we aren't mind readers and we do have to express ourselves to others. When my partner forgets to express his boundaries, I like to tell him how flattered I am that he thinks I'm psychic, but I haven't developed that skill yet! He laughs every time and says "Oh yeah! I forgot to communicate it!"

Some needs are less important to us than others, so when determining your boundaries, I would start by placing them in 2 categories: negotiable and non-negotiable.

I will give you a few suggestions:

Start by making a list of the most important relationships in your life. Beside each name write your wants and needs. Then write beside the needs: negotiable or non-negotiable. Sometimes we're not even sure about our own agreements so it is important to be clear. Here's an example of my agreements with others and myself:

Myself:
Working out every day: Negotiable (I can miss some days)
Meditating every day: Non-Negotiable
Cleaning the house: Negotiable (I can miss days when I'm tired)
Eating fruits and vegetables every day: Non-Negotiable

With my partner:
Speaking kindly to me: Non-negotiable
Quality time: Negotiable
Honesty: Non-negotiable
Affection: Negotiable
Loyalty: Non-negotiable

Oftentimes, we expect others to know what we need but everybody has different wishes and values. For example, in my relationship, my partner's required agreement is to have a set scheduled time to clean. One of my agreements is flexibility when it comes to organizing and cleaning the house. We both feel that this is negotiable, so when our wants clash, we can then talk about it and come to a compromise. Half the week his way, the other half my way! This way we both feel valued. When we don't tell others what we need we're not giving them the opportunity to respect our boundaries but most often people close to us do want to respect them.

When setting boundaries, I highly recommend you express them when you're feeling calm. This way your needs are clear and if they have any questions you may go into details if you want. When we state what we need after the boundary was crossed and we now feel disrespected, the emotional charge behind our words may not be what we are truly feeling. If you've never expressed a need to anyone, understand that when you do, it may come with resistance at first. I would suggest you simply just repeat the boundary. The same would happen if someone you've known for years suddenly approaches you with a new need. You may be confused and surprised, but it doesn't mean you won't respect it or at least be willing to compromise.

A non-negotiable agreement for both my partner and I, is loyalty. We have a zero-tolerance rule for infidelity and we both have the same consequence if that boundary were to be crossed. A breakup. Not everyone may share the same consequence of that boundary being crossed. I have clients that choose therapy as a consequence of infidelity.

When agreements are not respected and we've expressed our hurt and the person persists in disrespecting them, we then need to apply natural consequences. For example, if I don't show up for work, I will get a warning. A warning is my boss expressing his discontent. If I continue to not respect the office rules and overstep by not showing up to work over and over again, I will not get paid and eventually I may even get fired. Those are the consequences.

Let's say I didn't show up to work for weeks and my boss either responded by ignoring me or yelling but regardless, I still got paid. I may learn that all I have to do is endure a little yelling or ignoring without it affecting my paycheck or job. Yelling and ignoring aren't healthy consequences. You will encounter very respectful people who will return to work after the first warning, and thankfully those people don't need consequences since they are being considerate. Not everyone will respect the warning and that's when consequences are needed. The same thing applies to our relationships. If people disrespect our agreements after we've told them how we feel about it and they continue to do so, we need to apply natural consequences. A simple example in our home of 4, is my partner and I require the cat litter to be cleaned 4 times a week. We each have a turn on separate days. If one of us doesn't do it on our assigned day, the natural consequence is we have to then take over the next person's cat poop cleaning shift. Nobody wants to add work to their chores, so it is respected. This boundary is negotiable. We allow the kids to pick their days and we allow exceptions on exam and sports weeks. This allows our family to feel valued and respected.

Disrespected agreements should always come with consequences. If they refuse to respect them, that's when you can re-evaluate the relationship. Ask yourself are you willing to live with this if it never changes? If so, it may be a negotiable boundary, so perhaps communicate with the person by asking if they are willing to compromise. If not, perhaps ending the relationship may be the healthiest way to move forward. In the end, you must do what is right for you.

When you state your boundaries remember to talk about possible healthy natural consequences. Remember agreements are saying -I matter, my feelings matter. Everyone's feelings matter.

HOW DO I PROTECT MY ENERGY FROM NEGATIVE PEOPLE?

Our emotions and our thoughts hold energy, and oftentimes we can feel the energy of other people. But why is it that sometimes when we walk into a crowded room, we will feel drained especially if people around seem to have a "negative vibe"? Something about them feels "off" and we can sense it. We could be having a great day and as soon as we're in crowds or around certain people our energy gets depleted. What I try to teach my clients is instead of trying to avoid negative people and negative energy, try strengthening yours. When other people affect us, it means the influence of their feelings and energy is much stronger than ours, therefore it is overpowering. How do we strengthen our energy? I believe it is through awareness, compassion and recognizing our projections.

Loving all of yourself, meaning practicing self-compassion when you are feeling uncomfortable emotions. Removing self-criticism by working on loving the shadow aspects that you deem unacceptable. Growing your self-value, knowing you are worthy because you exist. I have some exercises we can do together later to strengthen your energy and build that love and worth. Empowering oneself through self-awareness can also be achieved by taking ownership of one's self-projections.

If I enter a room and perceive that everyone has a negative attitude, my conscious mind, which can only process 40 to 50 bits of information per second, will prompt me to avoid those individuals. However, my subconscious mind, which processes over 11 million bits of information per second, may be projecting my hidden negative emotions onto them without my conscious awareness. I may not recognize that I feel negative, as it could be an emotion that I suppressed and did not address and is now manifesting as I observe others. It's possible that something about these individuals triggered an emotional response, leading my logical mind to conclude that it's not me, but them who is responsible for the negative energy that I am sensing. Subconsciously a negative part in me is simply asking for my attention. The assumption is appearing in my mind. I am the one experiencing that thought, feeling and energy at that moment. Empowering our energy starts with learning to own the emotions that we are feeling.

If you notice someone seeming sad because they were displaying physical signs of sadness, for example, tears, a frown, and shoulders low. And to confirm this, you ask them, without opinions or judgment, if they are sad and they say yes, then you're simply stating a fact because they confirmed it. It is now a verifiable fact.

If you assumed, perhaps they are simply bringing a feeling that resides in you to the forefront. It doesn't mean that you are always negative. It can simply mean a small part of you, at that moment is negative and you can sense it in another.

To recognize an Emotional self-projection, you would ask yourself: Do I feel negative towards myself?

To recognize a Presumption self-projection, you would ask yourself: Am I feeling negative, or have I felt negative recently and I'm presuming others feel the same way I do?

To recognize a Knowledge self-projection, you would ask yourself: Am I assuming others can feel the negative vibes also?

To recognize an Absolved self-projection, you would ask yourself: Am I absolving myself of my negative energy, words, and actions and projecting it onto them?

There is a strange phenomenon that happens when you start owning your projections and emitting compassion. When you begin showing empathy towards yourself, you'll notice immediately that either the one person in that room that is kind and loving will approach you, or something will happen for the actual negative people to either leave or brighten up. If you don't believe me, test it out for yourself. Next time you catch yourself judging a person or a group of people, notice the feeling coming from your mind. Own your projections, give yourself compassion, and watch your reality shift!

In one of my meditations a few years back I received some information. This information download happens to me randomly and I don't have much of an explanation as to how this occurs. It is usually unpredictably about 30 minutes or so into a meditation practice. I call it a download because I feel like a computer that got information from a USB flash drive. A sort of feeling of being "plugged in" to a higher consciousness receiving loads of information within seconds.

Spiritual downloads are experienced by many people who refer to it as an experience of receiving insights or guidance from a Source Energy. Some believe that this Source is called the "Akashic Records." It can be described as a sudden influx of knowledge, ideas, or inspiration that seems to come from a place beyond oneself. I'm aware that to some of my readers, this may sound "nuts" and it may be strange to anyone who has not yet experienced it, but I can tell you, it's an interesting experience! Shared knowledge that we all can tap into when we take the time!

This being said here's something I "downloaded" a few years back:

We have 4 selves within us.

#1: The Conscious/Logic mind reading this now.

#2: The positive happy, excited, peaceful ego

#3: The negative sad, angry, anxious, and sometimes mean ego.

#4: The consciousness/ Observer

"The positive and negative are part of the human experience of duality and our conscious mind sometimes likes to say that one is good, and one is bad when in fact that's our logic trying to make sense of what makes us "feel good" and "feel bad." When we learn to connect with the #4 the Observer, we understand that "bad feelings" are not so bad when we accept them. The physical and emotional pain of the "bad stuff" is much easier to go through when you stop judging it and simply observe it."

It's important I mentioned these 4 selves so you can teach yourself to disconnect in a healthy way from your mind from time to time when you're feeling overwhelmed with emotions. Both the human experience and the consciousness are to be experienced to find that balance." To learn to connect with "the Observer" I would suggest everyday using the technique seen in chapter 2 -*hyperfocus on your senses.*

If you resonate with the download of the 4 selves, when you begin to recognize negativity within others or yourself, it's important to understand that there's nothing inherently wrong with having those thoughts or emotions. Any belief that negativity is inherently "bad" may simply stem from your conscious mind. If you feel uncomfortable with these thoughts, it's worth considering when you first learned to view them as bad. Once you take ownership of your thoughts and emotions, it's important to show compassion towards yourself and others. A crucial aspect of this is to offer love and acceptance towards the parts of yourself that feel negative. By doing so, you can let go of any judgment you may be carrying.

Sadness and anger need love to heal. The feelings are simply seeking validation. Many people in the world only want to focus on being positive, and although that is a wonderful concept, all that that's doing is pushing any negative feelings, thoughts, and beliefs into the subconscious. Just because we can't see the subconscious doesn't mean that it's not there. Remember the subconscious is processing a lot of information every second. You decide if you want to hide it from yourself or become aware of it.

There are exceptions to "negative" people affecting us. This is called "toxic negativity." This concept refers to a persistent and harmful attitude of pessimism, cynicism, or criticism that can have a detrimental impact on individuals and relationships. It is characterized by a pattern of negative thinking and behavior that tends to focus on the worst possible outcomes, exaggerate problems, and dismiss or undermine positive experiences and perspectives. Some people purposely try to go out of their way to hurt others. The way to differentiate those from self-projections is to show compassion. If compassion is met with love back, you know it was something "negative" within you. If your empathy is met with more hostility, it's time to set boundaries.

Let's say you're a student who consistently gets good grades in school and has a passion for learning. One day, you hear a rumor of a classmate who seems jealous of your success, spreading rumors about you to other students, saying that you cheat on your tests and don't really deserve your good grades. You believe they're doing this in an attempt to bring you down and damage your reputation. If you own your projections and meet them with compassion and they will meet you back with kindness, you may find out it was a misunderstanding, and you'll know you were making assumptions. But if they meet you with disrespect, you are not self-projecting, you're not assuming, you are stating a fact that this person is evidently being mean towards you.

Toxic negativity can manifest in several ways, such as constant complaining, blaming others for problems, distrust, excessive criticism, and self-sabotage. To overcome toxic negativity, individuals may need to engage in self-reflection and work on developing kinder thinking patterns, such as practicing gratitude, focusing on solutions rather than problems, and seeking out loving experiences and relationships. It may also be helpful to seek support from a mental health professional. It's important to remember that people who try to bring others down often do so out of their own insecurities and issues, and their behavior says more about them than it does about you. In these cases, remember to not own their projected, unhealed emotions.

"The most enlightened people in the world embrace their full potential of light and dark. When you're with people who recognize and own their negative qualities, you never feel judged by them. It's only when people see good and bad, right and wrong, as qualities outside themselves that judgments occur."
Deepak Chopra

CHAPTER 9

THOUGHTS CREATE EMOTION

Our brain receives information from the environment through our senses. This information is then processed in the brain, which creates a thought or interpretation about what is happening. This thought triggers an emotional response that corresponds to the interpretation we have made. For example, if someone sees a spider, their brain will process the information that may create a thought that the spider is dangerous. This thought will then trigger a feeling of fear, which is an emotion that corresponds to the interpretation they have made.

The way we interpret events is not only by our senses but often influenced by our beliefs, values, and past experiences. For instance, if we have a negative belief about ourselves or the world, we might interpret events in a more negative light, which can lead to more painful emotions. Our thoughts can also influence our emotions by impacting our physical responses. For example, if we think of stressful thoughts, our body may release stress hormones, which can trigger feelings of anxiety or fear. So, thoughts and emotions are closely linked, and the way we think about things can impact how we feel.

It is possible to become addicted to certain thoughts or patterns of thinking. This can happen when our thoughts become repetitive and automatic, leading to a habit of thinking that is difficult to break. If someone tends to have critical thoughts about themselves, they may find themselves constantly thinking about their flaws and failures, which can lead to a distorted self-image and feelings of worthlessness. This pattern of thinking can become a habit, making it difficult for the person to think lovingly or see things in a more balanced way.

Our brains can create neural pathways that reinforce repetitive and automatic thought patterns. Over time, these connections can become stronger, making it harder to break the habit of thinking in a certain way. Additionally, our assumptions about others and the world can be passed down from generation to generation, further reinforcing these patterns of thinking. Yes, I'm actually saying, some of your self-projections may have been passed on to you.

So how do we change our self-projections? We change our emotions. How do we change our emotions? We change our addictive habits. How do we change our habits? We change our thoughts! Awareness is the first step.

REPROGRAM YOUR MIND

Let's try a successful technique I use with my clients. On a piece of paper, jot down your answers to the following questions.

Awareness of projection:

1. What critical assumption have I made about someone? (adjective) *Ex: Dumb*
2. Have I felt this way about myself or others? *Ex: Yes, with myself*
3. Which type of self-projection may that be? *Ex: Emotional s-p*
4. What emotion surfaces when I feel this projection? *Ex: Sad*

Name the primary emotion:
Ex: Sad

Awareness of emotions:

1. When is this emotion most present within me? *Ex: Nighttime, before sleep*
2. What do I feel in my body when this emotion surfaces? *Ex: Stomach discomfort*
3. Have I validated my emotion, shamed it, or ignored it?

Ex: Ignored
4. What habits did I create from this emotion?
Ex: Comparing myself on social media

Name the primary habit: *Ex: Comparing*

Awareness of habits:
1. How often do I repeat this habit?
Ex: Daily, every evening
2. What benefits does this habit bring me?
Ex: Confirms my belief, validates my feelings
3. What small habit can I change to get started?
Ex: Self-loving affirmations before bed

Awareness of thoughts:
1. What thoughts have prevented me from changing my habits? *Ex: I'm not smart enough*
2. What new thoughts would I like to create?
Ex: I'm learning, I'm smart

Name the new emotion this thought may create:
Ex: Happiness
Name the new habit this thought may create:
Ex: Daily Affirmations
Name a new projection this thought may create:
Ex: Others are smart

You can do this technique as many times as you want, with as many thoughts as you want! It's important to practice this weekly or as often as you can so it can come naturally to you. What I mean is, imagine being invited to play basketball without any prior practice. Without practice, you are likely to struggle with dribbling, shooting, and passing. Similarly, it is crucial to regularly practice self-reflection and mental reprogramming, so you can develop the necessary skills to handle challenging situations with ease. Therefore, it is advisable to practice the technique regularly and not wait until a high-pressure situation arises. When the time comes, you will be well-equipped to manage your emotions and thoughts like an expert, just as a practiced basketball player can handle a game with confidence.

It is important to remember that changing your thoughts, emotions, and behaviors is a process that requires patience and dedication. Being patient with yourself and celebrating small victories along the way can help you stay motivated.

"Our beliefs control our bodies, our minds, and thus our lives..." Dr. Bruce Lipton

CHAPTER 10

OWNING OTHER'S SELF-PROJECTIONS

Do you sometimes second-guess yourself, wondering how others perceive you? If so, you're not alone. In a world where we're constantly bombarded with messages about how we should look, act, and be, it's easy to fall into the trap of worrying about what others think. But what if you could break free from this cycle and start living life on your own terms?

Introjection is when a person internalizes the beliefs and judgments of other people. This process can occur when we are exposed to external messages or cues, such as societal norms, cultural beliefs, or authority figures, and we absorb them without questioning or evaluating them. For example, a child may internalize the beliefs of their parents or caregivers without questioning them, leading to a sense of obligation to conform to their parent's expectations. This internalization can manifest in thoughts, feelings, or behaviors that reflect the beliefs of others, rather than our own authentic selves.

Introjection can be problematic when it leads to a loss of autonomy or a lack of critical thinking. If we internalize beliefs that are not in line with our own values or needs, it can lead to internal conflict, confusion, or a sense of disconnection from our true selves.

I grew up believing all the mean things people said about me. Over time this led me to not only internalize criticism but seek out further evidence to support my negative self-beliefs. For many years, I held the belief that I was "way too sensitive." Whenever a partner would walk away while I cried, it only reinforced my negative self-perception. I would often tell myself, "I'm too sensitive, that's why I always end up single." However, through years of projection work, I came to understand that these comments were simply reinforcing my self-criticism. As I became more aware of this pattern, I started to change how I viewed myself using shadow work. By doing so, I learned to no longer take criticism personally. Instead, I began to see it as an opportunity to reflect on my own thoughts and behaviors and make self-loving changes. This shift allowed me to break free from my dismissive self-talk and embrace a more peaceful and self-affirming mindset. We are only influenced by other people's opinions of us if we allow them to affect us. For instance, imagine you are wearing a RED top and jeans, and I begin criticizing your ugly YELLOW t-shirt, telling others how foolish it looks. While you might be bothered that I am not accurately describing your outfit, you wouldn't take it to heart. You wouldn't accept my opinion as true since you know you are not wearing a yellow shirt.

The same concept applies to our personalities. When someone criticizes us, it is up to us to decide if we will allow it to affect us. We may be upset that they are being unkind, but we do not have to internalize their comments about us. If someone were to call me "toxic" for example, it would not affect me because I do not feel that way. However, if someone were to judge a part of me that I consciously or subconsciously dislike, their comments would impact me more as they confirm my existing dislike for that aspect of myself. Hateful words are intended to hurt, belittle, or insult someone. They are often spoken with the intent to cause harm or damage to a person's self-esteem without offering any solutions or suggestions for improvement. They may not have any basis in reality which means they are self-projections.

Constructive advice is different from constructive criticism. Both are self-projections, but advice is typically delivered with empathy and consideration for the recipient's feelings whereas constructive criticism can be perceived as passive aggressive. Advice is given with the intention of helping someone learn and grow, rather than tearing them down. When evaluating feedback or comments from others, it's important to consider the intent behind their words. If someone is simply being mean or hurtful, their words are likely criticism without compassion. However, if someone is offering specific, actionable feedback with the intent of helping us improve, it's worth considering their comments and using them to grow and develop.

If we insist on giving a well-intended opinion to a person, it is also important to ask the other if they want our suggestions. If we are giving our opinion without consent it may not be well received. It can sometimes be challenging to tell the difference between constructive criticism and constructive advice, but there are a few things you can look for to help you distinguish between the two:

Consider why the person is saying what they are saying. Are they trying to hurt you, or are they trying to help you? Are they offering constructive suggestions, or are they simply being critical and mean?

Consider the tone. Hateful words are often delivered with a hostile, passive-aggressive, or insulting tone. In contrast, help is usually delivered in a calm, respectful, and empathetic tone. Evaluate the content. The feedback is usually objective, specific, and actionable. Hateful words, on the other hand, are often vague, personal, and not based on facts or specific behaviors. Ultimately, if you are unsure whether someone's comments are hateful or not, it can be helpful to ask for clarification. It's also essential to remember that you are in control of how you respond to feedback or criticism, and you have the power to choose how you allow others' words to affect you. If we all start owning our sh!t, imagine the world we could create. A world of accountability and inner awareness.

If we constantly search for ways to blame others for our own projections, we remain stuck in a state of bitterness and resentment. It's important to recognize and take responsibility for our own emotions and reactions, rather than constantly look for someone else to blame. Self-reflection and accountability can be uncomfortable, but it allows us to move past painful emotions and grow as individuals.

"When we see men of a contrary character, we should turn inwards and examine ourselves." Confucius

When others project their emotions onto us, we can learn to move forward by turning inward and saying: "How does this make me feel and what can I do about it?" It's important to approach self-reflection with a sense of compassion and understanding, rather than using it as a tool to beat ourselves up. Why did this happen, why am I like this? Why did I attract this? Why did I get sick? Why are some people lucky? Why did I get abused?

Humans have gained a lot of knowledge over the years asking "why" but I believe it should never be used to compare or shame ourselves. It is counterproductive to the self-love, and self-acceptance journey. When comparing ourselves to others, using the question "why" can be problematic because it often leads to self-judgment. Try using "why" for curiosity and learning but not for shaming. For example, when we ask, "Why we have not achieved the same level of success as someone else?" we are essentially questioning our own worth and value. Additionally, comparisons to others can be misleading, as we often do not have a complete picture of the other person's experiences or circumstances. It's also important to remember that each person's journey is unique and cannot be directly compared to others. Rather than focusing on comparisons, it can be more productive to focus on our own progress and growth and to set goals and priorities based on our own values and aspirations. This can help us cultivate a sense of self-compassion and self-acceptance, rather than constantly measuring ourselves against external standards. Instead of asking ourselves why we are not like someone else, we can reframe the question to focus on our own development, such as "What steps can I take to improve myself in this area?" or "What values and goals are most important to me and how can I work towards them?". This can help us shift our focus from comparison to self-improvement and personal fulfillment.

In this exercise, we will address both projecting onto others and accepting other people's feelings and opinions of you. This exercise is to help you become self-aware of your self-talk which can help increase self-understanding, reduce anxiety, and stress, and improve self-esteem. Self-criticism can impact your relationships with others, as you may project those emotions onto them. Becoming self-aware of your self-criticism can help you avoid this and communicate more effectively with others. You can become more resilient in the face of challenges and setbacks and be better equipped to manage difficult situations.

With a friend you trust: On a piece of paper, write about each other, something you dislike, or a behavior you would like them to change.

To find out which type you may be projecting from, ask yourself these questions:
Emotional self-projections: Have I ever felt the same way toward myself?
Presumption self-projection: What do I assume they feel, think, like, or dislike?
Knowledge self-projection: What do I assume they "should" know?
Absolved self-projection: What do I assume they do or act like that I may do or act like? Am I absolving myself of a projected behavior?

Now take some time to reflect on your thoughts and feelings. Ask yourself why you may be feeling a certain way and whether those feelings may be related to something from your past.

Only if you are both comfortable, share with each other your answers. This can reach a deeper layer of healing. When your friend tells you what they "feel" about you, I want you to become aware of the immediate physical feeling that this brings up within you. (This would be a good time to practice 3 in, 3 out, 3 all: *see Chapter 1 to review the full instructions for this practice.*) Write it down.

Now, what do you feel emotionally? Anger? Shame? Anxiety? Resentment?

If this hurts you, dive deep into why it does. Is this something that you already feel within yourself, and they are simply confirming it? Can you remember a time in your past when you first felt that feeling? Is this a label that you want to accept?

We get triggered when someone says something that accesses our subconscious feelings about something we already feel about ourselves. When you are aware of that feeling, ask yourself: Why do I believe this to be a "negative" trait? Can I change how I feel about this aspect of me? If not, do I want to keep believing this about myself? What other belief can I replace it with?

Here's an example: Partner says: You can be lazy.

If you feel hurt, it's because a part of you believes that to be true or at least somewhat true (on a subconscious level) and you don't like that you can be lazy, so you push it down to your unawareness.

Become the Observer: Ask yourself: Why is lazy "bad" to you? Perhaps you need to be lazy sometimes to regain your energy. Perhaps laziness is your body healing. Let's change the "lazy" belief to "recharging".

If you are not hurt by the lazy comment, it's because you already love and accept that part of you, or perhaps you are not lazy and they themselves are Absolved self-projecting a part of their subconscious onto you.

Question from social media:

__Anonymous__ How can I tell my partner he's projecting:

__Answer:__ This question makes me laugh because when I first started understanding and owning my projections, I would call out anyone who was projecting and boy oh boy did that backfire! Self-projections come from our subconscious minds, and they are very tough to recognize for ourselves so imagine, in the middle of a disagreement I dug into their bag (their unaware subconscious emotions) and showed them what they feel. I was met with resistance 100% of the time! I've learned over time when someone self-projects I simply say, "I don't feel like that's true for me, I hear what you're saying but I disagree." If they keep pushing, I sometimes ask them, "what makes you think that? Asking questions sometimes makes others self-reflect but if someone doesn't want to own their feelings, they will, unfortunately, do their best to place those feelings on you.

LABELS

It is human nature to use physical, emotional, and spiritual labels to understand ourselves.

There are many different types of labels, here are a few examples:

Identity labels: These are labels that describe a person's identity, such as gender, sexual orientation, race, religion, nationality, or political affiliation.

Behavioral labels: These are labels that describe a person's behavior, such as being introverted or extroverted, shy, or outgoing, aggressive, or passive, or responsible or lazy.

Diagnosis labels: These are labels used in psychology or medicine to diagnose mental or physical health conditions, such as depression, anxiety, OCD, autism, or ADHD.

Spiritual Labels: These labels often signal a person's beliefs, values, and practices related to spirituality or religion, and may also indicate a sense of community or belonging to a particular group or tradition, such as Catholics, Buddhists, Starseeds, astrological signs or Mediums.

Stereotypes: These are labels that are often based on assumptions or generalizations about a particular group of people.

Most of us need these to place ourselves in categories that we resonate with. Labels are important to humans because they help us to make sense of the world around us and organize information. Labels allow us to categorize and identify things, people, and ideas, making it easier to understand and communicate about them. When we label ourselves or others, we are signaling our belonging to a certain group or community, which can provide a sense of connection. Labels can help us to form social bonds and create a sense of shared identity with others who share the same label. However, labels can also be limiting and inaccurate. When we rely too heavily on labels, we may overlook the complexity and individuality of people and things. Labels can also be used to stereotype and discriminate against individuals or groups, leading to prejudice and bias. It's important to recognize the potential benefits and drawbacks of labels and to use them thoughtfully and responsibly. While labels can be useful for organizing information and creating a sense of identity, it's also important to recognize the individuality and complexity of people and things and to avoid stereotypes and prejudice.

It is okay to use labels when we are learning about ourselves. For example, I am an artistic, spiritual, Aquarius, woman. Each one of these labels resonates with me. Sometimes we feel lost, and labels help us find ourselves. I have a friend that discovered later in life she had ADHD. She struggled prior to finding out because she felt like she was "odd." After the diagnosis, she felt a huge sense of relief. She was able to validate, understand, and help herself because she resonated with that label. She made connections online with others that shared that label and has since made friends in her community and is helping others with ADHD.

Labels are empowering when used to discover who we are but there's a fine line between using them for understanding ourselves and using them as excuses. For instance, when we use it as a reason to treat people unkindly and then justify that the "label" is the reason for the unkindness. The use of labels to justify mean behavior is not a healthy or productive way to use them. Using a label like "neurodivergent" as an excuse for mean behavior is an example of "labeling theory", which suggests that individuals may internalize the negative parts of that label and behave according to them. While it is true that individuals with neurodivergence may struggle with impulsivity and emotional regulation, this does not excuse mean or hurtful behavior towards others. It is important to take responsibility for one's actions and seek appropriate treatment and support. It's also important to recognize that labels can be limiting and inaccurate and may not fully capture the complexity and individuality of a person. Using them to divide ourselves from others or believing that our "label" is better or worse than others can cause pain and separation. Some people do use them to compare themselves to others. For example, someone may use their socio-economic status as a label to feel superior if they are wealthy or have a higher social status, or inferior if they are poor or have a lower social status. It's important to note that labels can be limiting and don't define a person's entire identity or experience. It's also important to recognize and respect the diversity and complexity of individuals and communities beyond labels.

Labels can also become expectations. What I mean by that is when we are too rigid about our or others' identification, we form expectations on how we think those "labeled people" should be. When people categorize themselves or others based on labels, they often have certain assumptions or expectations about what that label means in terms of behavior, beliefs, values, and experiences. For example, if someone identifies as a feminist, there may be certain expectations about their beliefs and values regarding gender equality, women's rights, and social justice. These expectations can also lead to stereotypes, where people assume that all individuals who belong to a particular label or group share the same characteristics or traits. Those characterizations are usually validated with the reticular activating system. The system that acts as a filter for sensory information, allowing certain information to pass through to the conscious mind while filtering out other information. The R.A.S. does this by selectively activating certain neural pathways while inhibiting others. It does this by releasing neurotransmitters such as norepinephrine, dopamine, and acetylcholine, which can filter out information that contradicts our beliefs.

Many times, a label is so strong that we will take on that description unconsciously when we are around people who have those expectations. For example, if someone labels you as "lazy" or "unmotivated," you may start to believe this about yourself and behave in ways that reinforce this label. This can lead to a self-fulfilling prophecy where you become more like the label that has been assigned to you. It's important to challenge labels that don't resonate with us and to develop a sense of self-awareness and self-acceptance. This can involve reflecting on your values, beliefs, and experiences, and understanding how this shape your identity. It can also involve recognizing what labels you may be projecting onto others.

CHAPTER 11

HOW TO HEAL PAINFUL EMOTIONS

Inner child work is a form of self-exploration that involves accessing and healing the wounded kid within. The concept of the "inner child" refers to the emotional and psychological aspects of one's childhood experiences that have not been fully resolved or healed. It represents the parts of ourselves that may have experienced trauma, neglect, or emotional pain during childhood. These unresolved emotions and experiences can continue to influence our thoughts, behaviors, and emotions as adults.

The goal of this work is to provide a safe and nurturing space for the inner child to express their emotions and experiences, and to help heal any unresolved wounds. This can involve various techniques, such as guided visualization, hypnosis, journaling, art therapy, and role-playing. Individuals may revisit memories and emotions from their childhood and work to identify and heal any patterns of behavior or emotions that stem from those experiences. Through this process, they can develop a greater sense of self-awareness, self-compassion, and inner healing. This is usually done accompanied by a trained professional to uncover emotional wounds.

Since our critical self-projections come from our subconscious unhealed parts, inner child work can be beneficial to uncovering those wounds. It can be particularly useful for individuals who have experienced childhood trauma or emotional pain, as well as those who struggle with self-esteem issues, relationship difficulties, or feelings of emotional distress.

When working with my clients, I utilize a method called "Time Travel Reparenting." This involves leading them through a meditation exercise where they not only reflect on their past experiences, but also tap into their future selves. During the process, we employ visualization techniques to create a new, affectionate memory that feels genuine. This memory incorporates various versions of themselves from different points in time - past, present, and future.

Approximately six years ago, my attitude towards meditation underwent a significant transformation after attending a retreat. Previously, I only practiced meditation sporadically when I felt out of sorts, but after this experience, I began to treat it as a daily habit. I realized that meditation is comparable to brushing our teeth, in that the fresh feeling we experience after cleaning our teeth is akin to the mental clarity we attain after practicing mindfulness. Neglecting our dental hygiene can lead to "funky" breath and dental issues, just as failing to take care of our minds can result in anxious and depressive feelings. If someone who hasn't brushed their teeth in a while decides to start, they may require a dentist's assistance to clean their teeth thoroughly. Similarly, if someone hasn't meditated in years, may need guidance to get started. However, even after that initial guidance, if the habit of meditation is not sustained daily, the mind can become "funky" over time with emotions of stress. Consequently, I've dedicated the past six years to taking my meditation practice to a higher level, mastering the ability to sit with discomfort, transcending my thoughts, and even healing my body. It's been an exhilarating journey!

A few years back, I made up my mind to attempt a 3-hour meditation, which was longer than any I had ever done before. My intention was not only to test my ability to sit in a meditative state for that long but also to explore what kind of experiences would arise. After about an hour of meditating, I began to see swirling colors and felt as though I was soaring through space. Abruptly, my head jerked upward, and I found myself witnessing a memory from when I was 16 years old. I saw myself lying on my bed weeping. I remembered that day. I was contemplating ending my life and thinking of ways to do it. The "present me" could feel her pain and I started crying with her. In my trance, I walked over to her and gave her a big hug and told her how amazing her life will be. I told her to not give up because she was going to expect an amazing daughter and meet many wonderful loving people and live beautiful experiences. Simultaneously, I suddenly felt the presence of an older version of me, with my meditating body, guiding me through this process. So picture this: my present self was with my past self, and my future self was with my present self! If you were able to follow that and understand it, that wasn't even the trippiest part!

At the age of 16, I experienced a panic attack in bed, while contemplating ending my life. I was overwhelmed with emotions and cried for what seemed like hours until suddenly, in a split moment, my crying and hyperventilating ceased. It was then that I experienced an incredible feeling of love that surrounded my body. The sensation was so powerful that I even considered the possibility of it being an angel or some other supernatural force. When I started the meditation, I hadn't planned to visit the 16-year-old me, it just happened.

I have shared this story before and while some have suggested that this experience was purely subjective, it was such a profound experience that it inspired me to incorporate it into my coaching practice. By utilizing this technique, I have witnessed clients undergo a remarkable shift in perspective towards life. The incredible sense of unconditional love and validation that we feel is truly inexplicable. By doing this, a belief grows within us, the belief that we are never truly alone, and that we have always had our own support and love.

"Meditation means dissolving the invisible walls that unawareness has built." Sadhguru

TIME TRAVEL

If you're ready to try this meditation I will explain it here. I have guided meditations on my YouTube channel with music if you would prefer to try it that way. I've labeled them "Time Travel Meditations": @tanyabeautycoach

If you have PTSD or any emotional trauma that causes panic attacks, please check with your healthcare provider before practicing this on your own. If you're unable to try this, please skip to the next page.

Do you have a memory that still causes emotional pain when you think about it? If you feel comfortable doing so, take a moment to recall that memory. Sit with it for a moment but try not to let it overwhelm you.

Next, imagine yourself standing with the child version of yourself who experienced that painful moment. As you visualize yourself in that moment, consider what you wish your parents or caregivers had said to you at that time. Think about what words of comfort, validation, and support would have been most helpful to you. Take this opportunity to speak those words of comfort and validation to your child self. Say the things that you wish someone had said to you when you were going through that difficult experience. It can be helpful to visualize yourself hugging the little you or holding their hand in a comforting way.

Now try imagining yourself 5 to 10 years older than you are today. Using the same technique, picture the older version of you offering words of comfort and guidance for the present moment. Picture the older you gently placing their hand on your shoulder. Feel the presence of your future self. Listen to the message your older self has to tell you. Give your future self a hug.

You may even take this a step further and visualize all 3 of you together, holding hands. You are never alone, and you have the power to tap into something greater. Connecting with all versions of the deepest, most authentic part of ourselves allows us to access our inner wisdom, cultivate a sense of inner peace, and build deeper connections with ourselves and others.

After this practice, it is important to ground yourself as you return to the present moment. Grounding or earthing techniques aim to connect the body to the earth's electrical charge, which can help reduce stress, promote relaxation, and restore balance to the body. They are great to use after a profound meditation. Here are some grounding or earthing techniques you can try:

1. Walk Barefoot: Take off your shoes and socks and walk on grass, sand, or dirt. This allows your feet to make direct contact with the earth.
2. Forest Bathing: Take a walk in the woods or a park and immerse yourself in nature. Focus on the sights, smells, and sounds around you.
3. Gardening: Digging in the dirt and planting seeds can be a grounding experience. You can also connect with the earth by touching and smelling the plants.
4. Take a bath or shower: When you immerse yourself in water, feel the weightlessness of your body, and the sensation of water flowing over your skin.
5. Breathing: Focus on taking deep, slow breaths in and out, and imagine the breath moving through your body and down into the earth.
6. Visualization: Imagine roots growing from the soles of your feet and sinking deep into the earth. Feel yourself anchored and supported by the earth.

Remember that grounding and earthing techniques may work differently for everyone, so try different techniques and see what works best for you.

The Time Travel Reparenting exercise can be particularly helpful for those who are struggling to feel a sense of self-compassion, as it allows them to view themselves from a kinder and more objective perspective. It's important to understand that healing is not a one-time event. Just as we can catch a cold or flu multiple times in our lives, we may experience emotional setbacks even after we've made progress in our healing journey. This doesn't mean that we've done anything wrong; it's simply a part of the human experience. We cannot know health without sickness, just as we cannot genuinely appreciate joy and gratitude without experiencing their opposites. Taking the time to sit with painful memories and offering words of comfort to our inner child selves can be a powerful tool for healing. It's also important to recognize that healing is an ongoing process, and that experiencing setbacks or difficult emotions is a normal part of that process.

SPIRITUALITY AND SELF-PROJECTION

Self-Projection in the spiritual world is known as the Law of Correspondence. It is difficult to identify the first recorded person to talk about the universal laws, as these concepts have been present in various spiritual and philosophical traditions throughout history. Many ancient cultures and civilizations, such as the Egyptians, Greeks, and Hindus, had their own systems of beliefs and principles that includes ideas about the nature of the universe and its governing laws. One early example of the universal laws is found in the teachings of Hermes Trismegistus, a legendary figure in ancient Egyptian and Greek mythology who was credited with the authorship of a series of books called the Hermetic Corpus. These texts contain a collection of teachings about the nature of reality, the nature of the divine, and the principles that govern the universe.

The Hermetic Corpus includes the concept of the "Seven Principles," which are similar to the seven universal laws, and includes ideas such as the Law of Mentalism, the Law of Correspondence, and the Law of Polarity. The Hermetic teachings have been studied and practiced by various spiritual groups throughout history.

The law of correspondence is often expressed as "as above, so below; as within, so without." This means that the patterns and structures that exist in the higher realms of existence are mirrored in the physical world and that the internal state of an individual is reflected in their external reality. For example, the structure of an atom can be seen as a reflection of the structure of the solar system, with the nucleus of an atom corresponding to the sun, and the electrons orbiting around the nucleus corresponding to the planets orbiting around the sun. Similarly, this law suggests that the state of an individual's mind is reflected in their external circumstances. If someone has a loving and optimistic mindset, they are more likely to experience loving outcomes in their life, while someone with an angry and pessimistic mindset may experience more challenges and difficulties. This concept emphasizes the interconnectedness of all things in the universe and suggests that by understanding the relationships between different planes of existence, we can gain a deeper understanding of the nature of reality and our place in the universe.

I have experienced a few transcendental meditations that have given me a deep sense of inner peace and understanding about my connection to Earth, all beings, and the Universe. Some believe that people who experience similar encounters are lost in an illusion that the mind may be fabricating. Although that may be true, these experiences have released so much fear I used to feel daily. These unexplainable events bring me peace and help me release control. Whether it's real or imaginary, I'm ok living in the unknown, as long as I feel love.

I call myself an Earth Ambassador, meaning everything I do is for the Earth. If I can help elevate self-awareness and help people grow self-love, self-value, and inner peace, those people may self-reflect the next time they want to project hurt on someone. They may even pass that awareness down to their children. When we feel peaceful internally, we no longer feel the need to judge and criticize others. Loving people project love.

What used to be seen as pseudoscience is now being questioned!
In 2022, Alain Aspect, John Clauser, and Anton Zeilinger were awarded the 2022 Nobel Prize in Physics by the Royal Swedish Academy of Sciences for their pioneering experiments in quantum science. Their ground-breaking research on the "entanglement" state of tiny particles has laid the foundation for ultra-secure communications and complex computing and has highlighted the fundamentally strange nature of quantum mechanics. The Nobel committee explained in a press release that the three researchers conducted experiments that showed how multiple particles could be linked in such a way that changes to one particle would affect all others, regardless of their distance from each other. This concept of entanglement has important implications for the field of quantum computing and communications and has advanced our understanding of the behavior of particles at the smallest scale. This is scientific proof that we are all connected!

We are all connected to everyone and everything in the universe. Therefore, everything one does as an individual affects the whole. "
Dr. Serge Kahili King

Download I received during a meditation practice. I understand this part may not resonate with some people and that's okay! If it doesn't, you may skip to the conclusion but if it does, I hope you feel the love in my words <3

"Connecting to an awareness beyond our physical reality is the understanding that our consciousness is a bridge to a Source Energy within a unified field that we all share, where there is no up or down, high, or low. We are one consciousness. Different personalities of the universe experiencing itself. When we connect to our soul, we experience all. Separation becomes an illusion. Acceptance of the physical and emotional pain, pleasures, desires, and senses. We understand oneness. A clarity that I am all beings, and they are all me. I am both chaos and order, and chaos is simply a process of transition. I exist in everything and everything exists in me. We are using others as a mirror reflecting our subconscious feelings. The idea of self-projection in the realm beyond physical reality involves understanding that we are mutually experiencing one another, akin to multifaceted mirrors facing each other. To illustrate this concept, consider placing two mirrors in front of each other and witnessing the endless repetition of images. Now, envision a multitude of mirrors facing each other in all directions—above, below, and all around us— resembling a mirror maze found in amusement parks. The resulting view is boundless and infinite. In this way, we are like mirrors, constantly reflecting one another, extending our reach beyond the limitless expanse. When we understand self-projection not only from an emotional standpoint but a spiritual one, we can come together in love and unity, owning everything that is inside and outside of us. As within so without, as above so below."

CONCLUSION

I do want everyone to know, if you are not ready to become aware of your self-projections and face whatever lies in your subconscious, you have the right to feel that way. This is your life and your experiences. Many people are not ready to reach that depth of self-awareness and that's okay. Some don't believe we project, and that's okay too.

If you are on the healing journey and are on the path of self-discovery, I want to remind you it is not our job to instruct people or change other people's minds. It is our job to simply live our truth; if others resonate with that, they're welcome to join the journey. We cannot force anyone to acknowledge or even own their self-projections. By doing the work ourselves and owning our sh!t, we will over time lose judgment of ourselves and others, find inner peace, and this can set a great example.

As we come to the end of this book on self-projection, we are reminded of the power that lies within each of us. Through self-reflection, we can gain a deeper understanding of ourselves, our values, and our purpose in life. We are able to let go of limiting beliefs and patterns of behavior that no longer serve us, and instead embrace a more authentic and fulfilling way of being. But owning our sh!t is not always easy.

It requires us to be honest with ourselves, to confront our fears and insecurities, and to be   willing to make changes in our lives. Yet, as we have seen throughout this book, the rewards of self-awareness are immense. By taking the time to look within, we can tap into our inner wisdom, connect with our soul, and create a life that is aligned with our deepest values and desires.

So, as you continue your journey of owning your self-projections, remember to be patient and kind to yourself, to stay curious and open-minded, and to trust in your own inner guidance. Know that by doing so, you are taking a major step towards living a life that is truly fulfilling and meaningful. As you embark on your personal growth journey, take the time to recognize your accomplishments, learn from your mistakes, and stay committed to your goals. Believe in yourself, trust the process, and take action toward living your best life. It's never too late to start.

"Owning our self-projections is like holding up a mirror to ourselves, but it's not always a clear reflection. It's up to us to wipe away the fog and see ourselves for who we truly are, infinite potential"
Tanya Beauty Coach

ABOUT THE AUTHOR

Tanya Lena is a transformation and meditation coach who specializes in self-projection and time travel reparenting. She sees self-awareness as a crucial first step towards elevating consciousness and fostering compassion for others and the world around us. By helping individuals recognize the interconnectedness of all things and the importance of taking care of oneself and the planet, she hopes to inspire a ripple effect of loving change that will benefit all beings.

With many years of experience in the field of personal growth, spirituality, and transformation, Tanya has developed a unique approach to coaching that draws from personal experience, ancient wisdom, and modern techniques. Her clients have commended her ability to provide guidance and support that is both practical and profound, helping them to break through limiting beliefs and transform their lives in meaningful ways.

@tanyabeautycoach is a respected social media influencer and public figure. Her mission is to help individuals discover their true essence by becoming their own coach, tapping into the wisdom that lies within. In her role as a Gaia Ambassador, she has organized watch parties for the platform's members, who are all dedicated to exploring spirituality and personal growth. When she's not coaching, Tanya enjoys spending time with her family, in nature, with animals, practicing transcendental meditations, creating content, and connecting with her friends all around the world.

BIBLIOGRAPHY

Tuarez, Jaimar. "How Many Bits of Information Can the Brain Process? - NeuroTray." *NeuroTray*, 29 July 2022, neurotray.com/how-many-bits-of-information-can-the-brain-process.

Arts, The Behavioral. "Become IMPOSSIBLE to Manipulate! 6 Ways to Recognize and STOP Manipulation/ Gaslighting." YouTube, 29 Jan. 2022, www.youtube.com/watch?v=6B0tAn0nrJY&feature=youtu.be. Accessed 4 Jan. 2023.

The Shadow Effect: Illuminating the Hidden Power of Your True Self by Chopra, Deepak, Williamson, Marianne, Ford, Debbie(May 3, 2011) Paperback. HarperOne, 2023.

The Secret of the Shadow: The Power of Owning Your Whole Story. 1st ed., HarperCollins, 2002.

You Can Heal Your Life: Special Edition Box Set. Collectors, Hay House, 2009.

Psychology Today Staff, editor. "Gaslighting." Psychology Today, www.psychologytoday.com/us/basics/gaslighting. Accessed 4 Jan. 2023.

What the Bleep Do We Know. Directed by William Arntz, Betsy Chasse, Mark Vicente, 23 Apr. 2004.

Byrne, The Secret With DVD. Atria Books.2006

Sullivan, Will. "Breaking Down the Quantum Research That Earned Three Physicists the Nobel Prize." *Smithsonian Magazine*, 6 Oct. 2022, www.smithsonianmag.com/smart-news/breaking-down-the-quantum-research-that-earned-three-physicists-the-nobel-prize-180980900.

Printed in Great Britain
by Amazon

47702843R10106